Santa's Journey

Sharing Christmas Year Round

by

CLIFF SNIDER, BSC, MSC

ISBN 0-7414-4859-9

Published by:

INFI∞ITY
PUBLISHING.COM

1094 New DeHaven Street, Suite 100
West Conshohocken, PA 19428-2713
Info@buybooksontheweb.com
www.buybooksontheweb.com
Toll-free (877) BUY BOOK
Local Phone (610) 941-9999
Fax (610) 941-9959

Printed in the United States of America

Printed on Recycled Paper

Published September 2008

Dedication

This book is dedicated to my mother, Eva White,
for the love, encouragement and support she has
always given me. Merry Christmas Mom!

Acknowledgments

It is hard to describe the impact of everyone who has influenced my life and trying to pay tribute to all of them here would be futile, so please indulge my gratitude as I attempt to list some of them.

First of all, I want to thank Bob Snider and Eva Hunt for the union of their lives on Christmas Day in 1944 that brought about my birth three years later. Surely the choice of Christmas for your wedding day was somehow programmed into my DNA!

To my wife, Janie, I want to thank you for being my "reality check" in all areas of my life. It was your prayers that brought me to the acceptance of Jesus Christ as my personal Savior, and it has been your prayers that have sustained me ever since. Over the almost fifty years we have known each other, your smile has always warmed my heart. During our forty-two years of marriage, starting when we were both youngsters ourselves, you truly have been responsible for "raising Santa." Thank you also for your tireless efforts in helping me make sense of my own words.

I am sure my children, Carole and Rob, never dreamed their own Dad would become Santa Claus. Thank you both for embracing my role and allowing your children to believe in Santa. To my first granddaughter, Carrie Morgan Snider, I want to thank you for giving me a reason to become Santa Claus. You truly changed my life when I became your "Poppy Claus." To my other grandchildren, Maddie, Rachael, Robby and Daniel, thank you for being the incredible young people you are. I am so proud each of you believes in "The Real Meaning of Christmas" in your own heart.

To my *adopted* grandchildren Andrew, Allie, Billy and Abby, thank you for accepting me into your hearts as well.

I want to thank the incredibly talented artists I have had the joy of collaborating with. Thanks especially to Richard Tumbleston for putting me on the path of *The Artist's Way*. Thank you, Bob Timberlake, for welcoming me into your home as a young printing salesman and opening up the world of fine art to me. A special thanks is due to Ralph J. McDonald, a *real* Santa in your own appearance, for allowing me to be your Santa model. To Linda Cancel and Cara J. Reische, I hope we will continue our collaborations for many years to come. Thank you to Teresa Pennington, William Mangum, Doug Rowe and John Paul Strain for the special friends you have become. All of you have brought out the best I could offer; and, through your artistic talents, have created a Santa Claus far better than I could ever portray.

A special "thank you" is due to Wendy Leedy, the creator of the illustrations in this little book. Thank you for your faith in me when I presented my idea to you and my stories were in their rough stages. Your dedication to this project has truly been a blessing to me; I am honored to call you my "sister."

Thank you, Jimmy Tomlin, for bringing my journey to life in your newspaper and to the pages of *Our State* Magazine, and to the editor of *Our State*, Vicky Jarrett, thank you for your delightful letter introducing my story in your magazine and for writing the forward of this book. I am profoundly humbled by your kind words.

To the photographers who have used their own God-given talents to capture precious moments with the children I have met, I owe a special debt of gratitude. I want to pay a special tribute to my friend, Bryan Hayes, who gave me the gift of patience. To Terry Pardew, Tim Talley and Steve Norman, I look forward every year to our reunion as we bring Christmas to your patrons. To my new friends at B. and G. Photography, I look forward to many years of working with you and your clients. I also want to thank Harold Stroud, Bob Sterenberg and Steve Cash for helping me get started in my role.

Thank you to Tom and Holly Valent for your guidance and encouragement at the Charles W. Howard Santa Claus School, and to Tim Connaghan for your teachings in the International University of Santa Claus.

I also want to acknowledge my dear friend and Santa mentor, Ed Butchart, whose own book, *The Red Suit Diaries*, opened my eyes to the possibility that I, too, could one day become Santa Claus. Thank you also, Ed, for opening your home and your heart to me, and for believing in me.

Lastly, I want to thank my friend, Richard Harris, for the dream you have for Christmas Castle, and for choosing me to be a part of it. I hope we can share our mutual dream there for many years to come.

Introduction

You may ask yourself, "Why would a man desire to portray Santa Claus?" I am asked that question often. I believe those men who *truly* embrace the Spirit of Santa Claus have been chosen for the role. We are simple men who understand what it means to be a child again. To me, it is not the suit, nor the snow-white beard, nor the stature of a man that makes a Santa, it is the heart. As Santa, I have a deep yearning in my soul to get in touch with my own inner child and rediscover the gifts God has placed inside me. I believe God has placed unique gifts inside you as well.

I believe every child who visits Santa deserves to experience the true Spirit of Christmas; and since I don't believe in coincidences, I believe the children who come to see me have been sent by God. I want to be the light of God's love to those children. It's not even necessary to speak the saving message of Christ to them, although I will if the opportunity arises. I can be a messenger of love through my eyes, my voice and my ears as I focus my attention on each little one who sits on my lap.

Through the reading of my "journey," my prayer is that you would catch a vision of how God is working in your own life. Your gifts can be translated through any artistic endeavor you desire to pursue. If you allow God's creativity to flow through you, there is NO LIMIT to the impact you may have on other people's lives.

I don't believe God has a *Naughty and Nice* list in Heaven when it comes to His children. He sees the good

He has placed in each one of us. God is the biggest
optimist there is! He sees through all of our failings and
mistakes right into the goodness we are all capable of. If
we can be messengers of that goodness – that *"God-ness"*
if you will – then He will use each of us in ways that will
astound us.

Foreword

I met Santa yesterday.

It's not the first time, of course. My grandpa took me to see him when I was six years old and missing my two front teeth. We visited him at the local five-and-dime: Santa must do a lot of shopping.

And I had a near miss with Santa only the year before that − just missing a first-hand glimpse of him when he left a doll carriage for me on our front porch. Santa must be quick.

He's kind-hearted, too. When my son was about 2 years old and a little undecided about how close he wanted to get to the Big Guy at the mall, Santa just happened to walk by, put his hand on my son's head, and said "Merry Christmas, young man." That was just enough for my little guy.

Yesterday's experience, however, was different. It had been a full day of phone calls, appointments, and editing the stories for the December issue of the magazine. Needing to stretch my legs for a moment, I grabbed some papers to take to the art department. I stepped out of my office and right into the path of, you guessed it, Santa Claus, who was standing in the hallway before my very eyes.

On this particular occasion he didn't have on a suit of red fur trimmed in white, anchored by a shiny black belt. Nevertheless, it was easy to recognize him from his full white beard and mustache, a little on the curly side, as well as wire-rim glasses perched on his nose. Not so chubby and plump, but still a right jolly old elf − that was him, as though I had conjured him from the words of the story I had just finished editing.

For a moment, I had no idea what to say. "I've been good this year" (as appropriate as that may be with Santa Claus) seemed a little out of place for someone my age and in an office setting. So, I held out my hand, introduced myself, and said, "You must be Santa Cliff." As in Cliff Snider, perhaps the most Santa of them all.

As my acquaintance with Cliff has grown to a friendship, I've found that he has the heart of Santa. And more than that, he has a heart for Christ. Playing the part of Santa has become entwined with every facet of his life, including his faith, making this not only a character to play, but also a ministry of sharing God's love and grace to all he meets.

This story of how Cliff became Santa and the lives he has touched has warmed my heart, and now I'm sure it will yours as well.

Vicky Jarrett
Editor in Chief, *Our State* magazine

Table of Contents

Santa Receives His Mission

My dad loved Christmas! It was his favorite time of the year. He loved the music (especially the Christmas carols), the lights, the food and decorating our small house for the holidays. Every year Dad would have a family Christmas photo taken which he would then reproduce at his print shop for us to send to our friends and relatives. People would be so impressed to receive a custom Christmas card from us, as that was before personal photo cards. One particular card was a photo of my brother and me sitting in front of our fireplace with a plastic Santa Claus between us.

On Labor Day weekend of 1962, my dad and one of his brothers made a trip to Camp Lejeune Marine Base to pick up his brother's two sons, who had just gotten out of the Marine Corps. I remember Dad talking to me that morning before he left about how he really didn't want to be gone from us for the holiday weekend, but his brother wanted him to ride along. Dad couldn't drive, he never had, but he felt he could at least keep his brother company. So with reluctance he bid us "goodbye." That was the last time I would see him: on their return trip home, all four men in the car were killed in a head-on collision when a truck that had just passed another vehicle hit them.

I guess my childhood ended that Labor Day weekend as I realized I was "the man of the house" now, being the older brother. At 15 years old, I felt that I would have to take care of my mother and my little brother.

As Christmas came around that year, my Methodist Youth Fellowship group decided to provide a Christmas party for a mission church in our town, and they asked for a volunteer to be Santa Claus. People had always made fun of me for being overweight; so, almost as a joke, I was elected to be Santa. Deep down inside though, somehow, I felt like the fake beard and suit would cover up the hurting person I was inside; and if I could bring happiness to others, then maybe, doing so would fulfill the loneliness that had invaded my soul.

So, for Christmas of 1962, I put on a Santa Claus suit and made my "grand entrance" at the Beddington Street Mission in High Point, North Carolina carrying a hand-cut, cedar Christmas tree on my back, along with a big bag of toys. The rest of the youth group followed and helped the children make linked chains out of construction paper to decorate the tree. Later "Santa" passed out presents to the children while refreshments were being served. Little did I know that qualifying to be Santa because of my size, was the beginning of a lifelong ministry.

Forty-two years later, in 2004, I was interviewed by a newspaper reporter for a story in my hometown paper. During the interview, the reporter asked me if I thought my dad would be proud of me. Tears immediately welled up in my eyes because no one had ever asked me that question, and I had been afraid to ask it of myself. As I began to answer, I told the reporter the following story.

I had been invited to be Santa in Laurens, South Carolina by a dear friend who has painted several portraits of me in my Santa costumes. Not wanting to make the trip by myself, I invited my eight-year-old grandson, Robby, to go with me. With a father's wisdom, my son, Rob, suggested he would like to go too; he knew Robby would be a "handful" if I was by myself. The weekend was a wonderful bonding experience for all three of us.

One night while we were enjoying a bucket of chicken after a long day, Robby said to his father, "Just think, Dad, we've got Robert Clifton Snider the 2nd, 3rd, and 4th all together in one place for a whole weekend!" To that revelation I responded, "You know Robby, I feel like Robert Clifton Snider, Sr. is here too!" With that story fresh in my mind, I told the reporter, "Yes, I know my Dad would be proud of me."

Santa's New Suit

Did you ever wonder where our image of Santa Claus comes from and why he dresses the way he does?

Our modern version of Santa Claus was born out of the imagination of a classical and Biblical scholar. Clement Clarke Moore was a poet from Troy, New York who was accustomed to writing Christmas stories for his children. In 1822 he wrote, "A Visit from St. Nicholas," better known as "The Night before Christmas."

The poet's Santa was a chubby, elfin-like character who arrived in a "miniature sleigh, drawn by eight tiny reindeer." "He was dressed all in fur from his head to his foot," but instead of noting the *color* of his suit, he described it as "tarnished with ashes and soot."

Because of the author's familiarity with Dutch, German and Scandinavian folklore, his poem about Saint Nicholas was drawn from the Dutch tradition of "Sinter Klaas" (a holiday celebrated in Holland on December 24th and 25th.)

Moore's story, which had only been intended for his children's amusement, was anonymously published a year later in the *Troy Sentinel* and it was, in fact, many years later before the story was attributed to the author. His imaginary tale, reprinted countless times as "The Night before Christmas," has endured as a beloved part of American culture.

So how did Santa get his RED suit?

A young German-born New Yorker named Thomas Nast, a cartoonist for *Harper's Weekly*, began creating sketches of Santa Claus during the Civil War. He gave Santa the stature of a normal man and portrayed him as a jolly, plump, grandfatherly figure, dressed in a red suit with white ermine-fur trim. He had a pointed stocking cap, square-buckled shoes and a big wide belt. Nast also gave Santa a home, the North Pole, where he kept his big book in which he recorded all the names of the children who had been "naughty or nice."

In the earlier years, as the "Santa season" neared, I would rent a Santa Claus suit with a wig and beard. I laugh now as I think of how hot I was with all of that costume on, especially since I lived in North "Pole" Carolina! When I made my entrance from the cold outdoors into a warm room, my breath (coming from under the beard) would immediately cause my glasses to fog. For several seconds, I couldn't even see where I was going!

After more than thirty years of renting costumes when needed, a friend recommended I read a book titled, *The Artist's Way: A Spiritual Path to Higher Creativity*, by Julia Cameron. One chapter suggested you pursue your own creativity with all the authenticity you can think of. By this time in my life, I had my own beard which I kept trimmed short. I thought, "Why not let my beard and hair grow out more so I don't have to wear a wig and artificial beard anymore?" It seemed like a revelation, but it was actually just common sense.

About that same time, I saw a friend in town who had played Santa Claus for the local Rotary Club. He had the most beautiful and authentic suit I had ever seen. When I asked him where he got such a nice suit, he told me about the Santa Claus Suit and Equipment Company, now located in St. Clair, Michigan. I thought, "You mean there really is a place where Santa gets HIS suits made?"

My next challenge was to figure out how to get a suit like that for myself. After all, it was really expensive. So I thought about it and figured I could ask my mother for it as her Christmas gift to me. "After all," I remember thinking, "Mom will understand how much it would mean to me and do everything she can to see that I get it." (I was just as certain my wife would not understand spending that kind of money on such a thing.) At the time, a "one size fits all Santas" wouldn't work, so a custom-made suit was ordered.

I still wear that suit, even though I have added several others to my wardrobe. Every time I put it on, I think of the unconditional love of my mother who wanted the very best for her son.

I have personally added a special significance to the colors of Santa's suit. To me, the red of Santa's suit represents the color of the blood Jesus Christ shed when He gave up His life as a sacrifice for my sins. The white fur represents how clean I am washed when I accept the forgiveness of my sins through believing Jesus died for me. As His representative, I can proclaim the forgiveness God offers anyone through belief in His Son. I can also proclaim the gifts God wants to give us as His children, because like any parent, He only wants the very best for each of us.

Santa's Special Friend

I once read somewhere that, as Santa, you should go where you are celebrated, not just tolerated. That is good advice on which to build my Santa career. There is not a happier place on earth for me to be than in the presence of young and old alike who believe in Santa Claus and enjoy meeting him.

One of those people was Bryan Hayes, a young photographer I met around 1995. Bryan was trying to start his own photography business and his mother, Vickie, let him use the back room of her catering business, Create a Cake, in Greensboro, North Carolina as a studio. Bryan contacted me and asked if he could take my photograph as Santa for his portfolio. I was flattered, because, while I had paid other photographers to do promotional photos of me, no photographer had ever invited me to be his model.

At our first meeting Bryan explained that he had an anxiety disorder that made him uncomfortable working with people, but he assured me if I would be patient with him, he would get some good photographs. Then I watched a true artist go to work. Behind the camera he was as confident as any master photographer would be. I could tell he instinctively knew the exact right moment to snap the shutter. Before long the entire day had passed and I knew we had gotten some really great material.

As was customary back then of a master photographer, Bryan liked to develop and print his own photographs and would hand-mount his custom prints. After a few weeks he called and invited me to come see the results of his work. I couldn't believe my eyes. I was actually looking at photographs of Santa Claus – as real a Santa Claus as I had ever seen – and it was me!

Bryan's face beamed as I carried on about how wonderful his work was. His mother encouraged him to show some of her bakery clients the photographs; soon he had a waiting list of customers wanting their own photographs with Santa the next Christmas. Bryan sheepishly asked if I would let him use me as *his* Santa for photographs with his patrons. My response was, "Are you kidding? I want to bring all of my grandchildren to you to have their photos taken with Santa too!"

I thought the next Christmas would never come; actually, I feel that way every year, but I was especially anxious for Christmas of 1996 to come around. At the time, I had four grandchildren. Carrie Morgan Snider, my *real* reason for becoming Santa," was five years old, Madeline Noëlle Keefer was three, and her sister, Rachael Caroline Keefer was two. My namesake, Robert Clifton Snider IV, had just been born in October of that year.

The photographs Bryan created with children were equally spectacular to the ones he had done of Santa alone the year before. Of course, I was even more excited since now I had photos of my own grandchildren sitting on my lap to prove I WAS Santa or "Poppy" Claus to them. Bryan was indeed a master at his craft, and each client received the same patient and meticulous attention that had become his trademark. I found myself learning from him as he taught me to be patient too. I am not a loud, demonstrative "ho-ho-ho Santa." My usual calm and quiet demeanor seemed to put our visitors at ease. In a few weeks he called again and said he had the results for us to look at, and once again his talent was obvious.

The next year Bryan's mom was catering a corporate dinner at Brian Park in Browns Summit, North Carolina and Bryan asked if Santa could come to be photographed with each guest. I was delighted to oblige; after all, now I was being compensated for my appearance. This would be the first of many parties I would attend at Brian Park, and Bryan Hayes was right there directing the photography with his usual skill. At this first party, his mom had rented a beautiful sleigh for Santa to sit in with his guests and one of her coworkers had even dressed up as "Mrs. Claus." This was another first for me because I had never had my picture taken with "Mrs. Claus." Bryan's photograph of us together is another one of my favorites.

November 26, 1998 was my mother's 80th birthday. My brother and I decided to plan a surprise birthday party for her, so we rented a banquet room at a local hotel and sent invitations to Mom's closest family members and friends. We also invited Bryan Hayes to be our family photographer for the evening. Nearly fifty people joined in our celebration and I was proud to have Bryan among us. Afterward he prepared a handsome family album to help us remember the evening forever.

That was the last time I saw Bryan Hayes. I later heard from a friend that he had decided he could not support himself through his photography alone, so he had gotten a full-time job. On his first day to report for work, he suffered an anxiety attack in the parking lot of his new employer. He was taken to the hospital and his parents, who were on vacation, were called to come home. At the hospital, his parents were told by their family physician, which had treated Bryan all his life, that he would be fine after a few days rest in the hospital. Sadly however, Bryan passed away later in the week at the hospital.

We can never explain why some people are taken away before their time. Bryan's story reminds me of how short life can be and helps me to not take my own health for granted. Right now, as I write this story, I am recovering from total hip-replacement surgery. It is my goal when I turn sixty this summer, to be in better shape than I have been in a long time.

Hardly a week goes by that I don't think about my friend, Bryan Hayes. He is one of the many people who opened the door of creativity I now enjoy so much. His photographs have become the source of several portraits other artists have painted of me. I know that would please him greatly. But mainly, it is his quiet and gentle spirit that remains in my memory. Someday, I hope people remember me in the same way.

A Red Kettle Santa

I have always associated the red kettles the Salvation Army distributes to retail locations with Christmas. When I was growing up, I remember seeing Santa Claus ringing the bell while standing at a Salvation Army red kettle and wishing everyone a Merry Christmas.

When I became Santa Claus, I thought one of my activities should be to volunteer to ring the bell for the Salvation Army. How surprised I was to find out that, in some areas, Santa is not "politically correct" for such an assignment. I belonged to a local Rotary Club whose members volunteered to ring the bells at Christmas, so I was assigned my slot of time. I then contacted the Major in charge of the local Salvation Army unit and asked if I could man my post as Santa Claus. He was delighted for Santa to add his good wishes to everyone, so he eagerly agreed.

My first year of ringing the bell was at the local Wal-Mart. Upon arriving for my turn, I created quite a stir with the shoppers as I approached the entrance of the store. Even though it was a cold, brisk night, I was quite comfortable in my wool Santa Claus outfit, complete with hat, gloves and red long johns.

You can carry out an interesting study of people by watching how they approach or avoid the Salvation Army kettle. Most people are good-natured and friendly as they pass. Some will make a small donation, or will promise to stop by when they leave. A few will even slip a dollar bill or something larger in the kettle. Almost everyone was excited to see Santa at the kettle and would at least stop to talk, especially the children.

The thing that fascinates me, though, is the trouble some people will go through to avoid going near the kettle. Some will even pry the exit door open, so they won't have to pass by it. Avoidance is for them to rush by without so much as a "hello" or "Merry Christmas," with their head down, trying to avoid eye contact.

So, there I was, ringing the bell and wishing everyone a "Merry Christmas" and "ho- ho- ho-ing" until I was almost hoarse, when all of a sudden a man stopped about ten feet in front of me and yelled, "You're not the meaning of Christmas! Jesus is the meaning of Christmas!" Wow, I looked at him, ready to make a response, because I KNOW Jesus is the true messenger of Christmas and He lives inside my own heart! I was looking forward to sharing that fact with the accuser, but he escaped into the store before I had a chance to agree with him.

During my entire career as Santa Claus, I have endeavored to represent the Christ of Christmas to everyone I come in contact with, especially the children. It is my opinion that because children trust Santa Claus, he has the opportunity to present them with the simple truth of Christmas, that God sent His most special gift at Christmas. It makes perfect sense to them. I consider it my sacred duty to be the representative God intends me to be when I wear the red suit. However some don't want to hear *my* side of the story. That particular night, I have to admit, I had to push back some hard feelings toward such an accuser; and it was a little difficult to pray for his understanding, but I did.

Since then, I have had other accusers, and people who just didn't believe in the spirit of Christmas through the person of Santa, or anything else for that matter. I have learned to love them all and respect their right to have opinions and beliefs different than mine. Santa must be the same to everyone, even those who differ with him. After all, isn't that the way we all are supposed to react? Wasn't it Jesus who said, "Love your enemies, and do good to those that persecute you?"

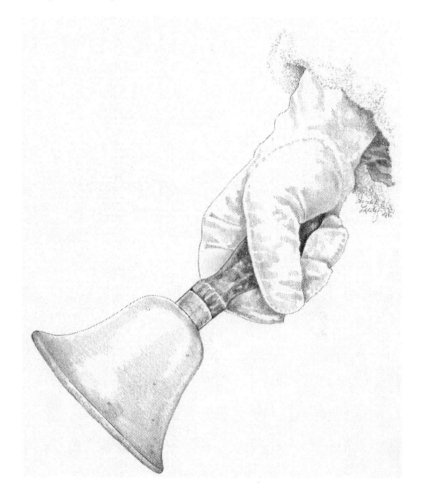

Jeffrey's Present

It was while ringing the bell for the Salvation Army that I was offered my first job as a *real* Santa Claus. I was standing in front of the local Wal-Mart greeting customers on a cold December night when a lady stopped at my kettle and said, "You are the most real-looking Santa Claus I have ever seen!" I thanked her and told her I appreciated the compliment. As a result of our chance meeting, Phyllis Hendrix, of Hendrix Batting Company, became my first Santa client and has since become a dear friend. I enjoy visiting with her and her employees every year. I have seen many of the children there seemingly grow up right before my eyes.

My visit in 2002 was especially memorable. I arrived early, so I decided to have dinner with everyone. As I walked in, I noticed a little boy at the buffet getting only shredded cheese on his plate. He asked if I could help him, so I began small talk with him, asking if he liked cheese and if it was all he was going to eat. He told me his name was Jeffrey and invited me to sit with his family.

After escorting me to the table, Jeffrey politely helped me take off my coat and placed it over the back of my chair, like a little valet. I took my gloves off while he held my chair for me to sit down. As we enjoyed our dinner together, he asked all sorts of questions about my reindeer, the North Pole, Mrs. Claus, and how I got there. He asked so many questions that his grandmother finally had to tell him to "Let Santa finish his dinner, Jeffrey."

After a wonderful meal topped off with a piece of pumpkin pie with real whipped cream, Jeffrey helped me put my jacket, gloves and hat back on. Then he led me to my chair next to a big beautiful Christmas tree. As he helped me get situated, all of the children came crowding around us. When Jeffrey asked me if he could be first, I told him I didn't know who the presents were for, and he would have to wait his turn while I called out the names. After seeing his look of disappointment, I asked if he would be Santa's special helper, since he knew all the children. He could help me find each child so I could give them their gifts and listen to their Christmas wishes.

So, one by one, I called the children up to receive their present from Santa. Young children as well as the older ones were delighted to sit on Santa's knee and tell me what they wanted for Christmas. I could tell Jeffrey was getting a little anxious as to whether or not there would be a present for him, but he remained hyperly patient. He offered me a drink of water from time to time and then carefully put the glass on the table next to my chair. Upon another child's name being called, he would enthusiastically announce their name to the crowd. Finally, there was only one present left and Jeffrey looked concerned. I slowly picked up the package, looked all over it for his name, and finally found it. I was beginning to wonder what in the world I would say if it had not been for him. When I called his name, he literally jumped into my lap. He was so relieved Santa had not forgotten him.

As I had done with each child, I asked Jeffrey what he would like Santa to bring him for Christmas. He told me all he wanted was a fire truck, a specific kind. "I want a remote control fire truck with a ladder that goes up," he replied. I told him I would see what I could do, thanked him for being such a great host and helper and then slid him off of my lap so he could open his present. As he tore into the wrappings from the package (that was nearly as big as he was), what should appear but the biggest, shiniest, remote control fire truck I had ever seen! Jeffrey squealed with delight as he ran back to me, threw his arms around my neck, thanked me and said, "You did it! You brought me just what I wanted! You knew it all the time! Thank you, thank you, and thank you!" I was as surprised and delighted as he was!

What a wonderful gift that was for me, because you see, I don't believe in coincidences. My role as Santa Claus was authenticated in my own heart, by my belief that God made sure the last package contained exactly the toy the last child had requested. I believe God led me to Jeffrey that night because He knew Jeffrey needed a reason, a sign, to believe in Santa Claus...and so did Santa!

Pop Pop's Violin

My grandfather, William Wyatt Snider, moved to High Point from nearby Denton, North Carolina when he was 26 years old. He bought a corner piece of property on Green Street where he built a house for himself and his new bride. There, he raised his family of six boys and two girls.

W. W. Snider, better known as "Pop Pop" to us grandchildren, was always a quiet, gentle Christian man. My father once told me that one day, while helping his father with a project, he lost his grip on a piece of lumber and the board struck his father on the side of his head. As blood ran down his cheek, the elder Snider uttered no stronger a complaint than "Shucks."

My grandparents manifested a Christian devotion, reflected in a family which, to this day, continues their dedication to home, church and community. When I was younger, it was inspiring to see my whole family; grandparents, parents, five uncles, two aunts and their children file into their pews at Wesley Memorial Methodist Church in High Point. The family would eventually grow to more than forty members occupying three pews on each Sunday morning.

I remember my grandfather as a self-sufficient man who only asked for the opportunity to do honest work. His first job when he came to town was with Snow Lumber Company. He worked as a glazier, putting windows in people's houses. He worked hard, saved his money, invested, and ventured into insurance and became a property owner. All eight of his children graduated from college. He watched them, with pride, extend the same spirit of usefulness into the community where his family name became synonymous with civic service and devotion.

One of the things I remember most about Pop Pop was that he loved parties, especially at Christmas. It was tradition for his entire family to gather at his house every Christmas for a holiday party. Uncles, aunts, and cousins would all congregate until the home would be running over with family members. One of my uncles had a movie camera and each year he would take home movies of the family reunion. Then, the following year, we would all gather again and watch the movies he had taken in previous years. It was fun to watch how we all changed from year to year as the family expanded, in more ways than just the numbers.

Pop Pop also had a tradition of having an annual Sunday lunch during the Christmas season with all of his sons and grandsons; no women allowed. It was almost like he was passing his patriarchal blessing on to his sons. The location for this meal was always the dining room of the old Biltmore Hotel, an impressive pre-Civil War roomery that stood by the railroad tracks in downtown High Point.

The Biltmore was famous for its family-style dinners. Heaping plates of fried chicken, country ham, mashed potatoes, green beans, sweet corn, coleslaw and hot gravy would be served on tables covered with crisp, white, starched tablecloths and real-cloth napkins. But to me, the highlight of the whole meal was the home-made yeast rolls that were so light they almost floated off of the platter. With a pat of real butter, I thought I was in Heaven.

At the particular dinner I remember, I had the honor, for some reason, of being seated to the right of Pop Pop at the head of the table. It was understood that no one would begin to eat until all the food was served and Pop Pop had said the blessing. Then he was always allowed to serve himself before passing the food to the rest of us. Well, on this memorable day, the rituals had been completed and Pop Pop reached for the mashed potatoes first. He put a generous amount on his plate and immediately took a bite. I intently watched as his face grew red, his eyes began to water, and before I knew it, he spewed mashed potatoes all over me, my brother and anyone else within range. As I sat there in shock, he turned to me and said, "You know Sonny, a fool would have swallowed that!" The whole room broke into laughter, including me as I wiped potatoes from my face with my cloth napkin.

Such are the memories my kind grandfather left me with when he passed from this world at the ripe old age of 93. A year or two after his passing, one of his daughters was disposing of some of his belongings and she called me to ask if I would like to have his old violin. Being a violinist myself, I couldn't believe I had missed such an important detail of his life! My grandfather and I shared something more than relatives.

Upon receiving the old violin, at first I wasn't impressed with it. All of the hair was gone from the bow, the end peg that held the tail-piece in place was about to pull out, and the body of the violin was cracked in several places. I graciously accepted my aunt's thoughtfulness and after she left, I put the instrument away in a closet with my own violin and forgot about it.

In the summer of 1996, I began having severe health problems that eventually caused me to be hospitalized. After undergoing surgery, and receiving many prayers of family, friends and even my Christian doctors, God performed a healing miracle in my life.

While I was recovering in the hospital, I wrestled with a lot of issues going on in my life. I was miserable in my job, concerned over the welfare of our son and his daughter and, in general, wondering in what direction my life was going.

It was then, while flat on my back and helpless, I got the impression God wanted me to become more involved with playing the violin in our church praise team. I've never considered myself a musician, but I do consider any talent I have to be a gift from God. It was as if He was telling me to let Him be the bow, and I would be His violin.

Christmas was not far away, and as soon as I was strong enough, I went to the closet that had held my violins for many years. I took Pop Pop's violin out and tuned up the strings that had been silent for maybe fifty years. I got the bow from my own violin and, as I began to play, the sweetest music came from the old instrument. It was as if my family's entire heritage was in his violin. I could *see* my dad conducting a "ghost orchestra," as he would often do when he listened to great music. I could also *see* my grandfather playing his fiddle that I never knew he played. I *heard* God's voice in every note that came out of Pop Pop's violin.

In the process, I understood, for the first time, that I didn't have to be an accomplished musician in order to praise God. All He wanted from me was the intimacy that exists between a violin and the bow; otherwise, one would be silent without the other.

Since that day, my heart and soul have been overwhelmed with God's goodness and mercy, and my praise to Him has been transformed. I have also been given a love for my brothers and sisters on our praise team that I can't begin to describe.

Santa Finds a Bride

I first met my wife-to-be when we were in the seventh grade. We were only twelve years old at the time, so we certainly didn't consider ourselves as romantic interests. Our home-room teacher, Miss Coley, at Ferndale Junior High School, selected me to be in charge of creating bulletin boards for our class. For Christmas that year, I chose Janie O'Ham to help me. I found out she was quite an artist. She drew Santa Claus standing next to a fireplace with stockings hanging on the mantel, and I drew three robed choir boys singing Christmas carols. This "work of art," drawn on simple Kraft paper, would later adorn Janie's living room as a holiday decoration for several years.

We also began playing in the school orchestra together that year, Janie as a cellist and I as a violinist. Our friendship, born while working on a school bulletin board, and nurtured through music, was almost prophetic.

In 1964, Janie and I were finishing our junior year in high school. We had remained friends, getting to know each other more throughout the years. The orchestra played for the evening graduation commencement and I offered to give her a ride home. One thing led to another and we had our first date that summer.

Her parents only agreed to let us date by going to church at first. (That was one way they kept an eye on their six daughters.) Her church was a new experience for me, since her family belonged to a Pentecostal Holiness congregation. I remember being really apprehensive the first time I attended one of their services. It was definitely a big contrast from what I had grown up in. But I also figured, since they had church up to three times a week, we might be able to see each other quite often. It wasn't long before I actually began paying attention to what was being said. (Looking back on it, I guess I liked her more than I realized.)

My father had been a printer and I had worked in his print shop ever since I was twelve years old. (I still have my first pay slip when I earned forty cents an hour!) After Dad died, I continued my part-time job and even decided I wanted to go to college to learn the printing trade. The only four-year, degree granting, graphic-arts college was over 800 miles away in Rochester, New York. I was accepted into Rochester Institute of Technology and began my college career in 1965. Janie decided to stay home to attend Guilford Technical Community College.

Rochester could have been the North Pole as far as I was concerned. Since the school was located right on the banks of Lake Ontario, I thought my mother had dropped me off at the top of the world. When she left to return home, I felt like the loneliest person in the city. My dormitory room was in an old hotel downtown called Nathaniel Rochester Hall. My room was on the 14th floor and in the winter, when the wind would blow off of the lake, I thought I could feel the whole building shake. It was always so cold outside that my roommate and I used the window ledge of our dorm room as a refrigerator, hoping things would not freeze or fall off! My first year there I experienced over five feet of snow which was a big change from the average five inches in my home in North Carolina.

To me, Rochester was a magical city at Christmas. I secured a part-time job in a book bindery in the old part of town and rode the city bus from my dorm to work and back. From the bus stop, I would walk past the department store's windows and marvel at the huge display windows all lit up and decorated for Christmas.

Like many freshmen, the adjustment to college life was difficult for me. Being incredibly lonely, and rather shy, it was hard for me to make friends. I became active in several campus organizations, including a service fraternity. Unfortunately those activities took away from study time, causing my grades to suffer. I left school that first year on probation, unsure whether or not I would be returning.

That summer, I asked Janie if she would be my wife and return to Rochester with me. Happily, she agreed and, although her parents were reluctant at first (because we were so young), they gave us their blessing.

My summer job at Snider Printing Company was waiting for me, so I printed our wedding invitations and some "at home" cards to enclose. Our friends were really impressed with our "Park Avenue, New York" address. Little did they know our three-room apartment had less than 400 square feet and was in the back of our landlady's home!

My other part-time job was delivering flowers for my aunt's florist, which was next door to our print shop. She graciously helped me arrange the flowers for our wedding.

Janie asked a close friend to be her maid-of-honor, and that friend's mother made the gowns for the wedding party. By the end of summer, we had created a "do-it yourself" wedding with Janie's brother-in-law and my pastor pronouncing us man and wife. Afterward, we loaded all our accumulated, family hand-me-downs (along with wedding gifts), and headed back to New York.

Now, I was a "man on a mission," with a new wife and companion who gave me a purpose to work toward. I needed to complete my education in order to support my wife and the family we hoped to have. I truly was a happy new husband.

"Are You Santa's Brother?"

Several years ago I was having dinner in a restaurant with my wife. Christmas had been past for only a few weeks, so it was still fresh in most people's minds, especially those who "believe."

A family of three was dining nearby. The daughter, who must have been six or seven years old, kept looking in my direction and smiling. I acknowledged her, but was a little self-conscious because she kept watching me and then talking to her parents. The more she talked, the more animated she became until her smiles became an occasional wave, followed by a giggle when I would wave back.

We finished our dinner and as we were leaving, the little girl stopped me with a question, "Excuse me Sir, are you Santa's brother?" I broke out in my heartiest Santa laugh and replied, "What a polite young lady you are! Your parents have taught you so well! Why, Jessica, do you think I look like Santa Claus?"

With that response, her eyes grew wide as she exclaimed to her parents, "See, I told you he was the one, I told you he was Santa Claus, he even knew my name!" Her parents were as surprised and delighted as she was.

Knowing much more conversation might spoil the magic, I wished them all a "Merry Christmas" and left, without their realizing that Jessica's hair band had her name on it! In a special place and time, the magic and wonder of Christmas and Santa Claus had been kept alive for a little girl and her family.

Reflecting back over that special time, it occurred to me that God knows each of our names and loves us far more than we could ever know. I first became aware of that in May of 1970. My boss invited me to attend a Billy Graham Crusade in Spartanburg, South Carolina. Not wanting to offend him by declining his invitation, I agreed to go.

The crusade was being held at the First Baptist Church of Spartanburg, and Dr. Cliff Barrows, Dr. Graham's assistant, was the evangelist. At the end of the service, Rev. Barrows gave his personal testimony of how Jesus Christ spoke to his heart and said, "Cliff, God has a wonderful plan for your life." Suddenly, all of the things I had heard in Janie's church flooded my mind as I realized my own need for salvation.

My heart leaped right into my throat as I felt God was speaking directly to me as the evangelist continued. I honestly don't remember another thing Cliff Barrows said, but I knew God had taken that moment on May 23, 1970 to speak to me. I knew I needed to give my heart to Jesus so He could reveal what His plan was for me.

Further reflection on Jessica's story reminded me that I do have a brother…his name is Walt. Walt has a true Santa's heart with the stature and a wonderful deep voice to go with it.

Once I became a Christian, I began praying for Walt and tried to share the gospel with him. We lived apart and our lives were very different, so we rarely got together.

Through addictive habits that influenced his life in various ways, Walt eventually became a captive of drugs and alcohol. He went into a full-blown manic-depressive state which led to his involuntary commitment into a mental facility and tragically, the breakup of his marriage.

Thanks to wonderful and compassionate care from psychiatric and medical doctors, Walt conquered his addictions and came through that darkness in his life. He found a new career, a new bride, and a new home.

As years passed, I remember praying for Walt from time to time, fearing the lifestyle he was developing might, one day, tempt him again to give in to the demons that had once controlled his life. I tried to witness to him periodically about how Christ loved him and had a plan for his life.

Regretfully, I eventually quit praying for my brother, and even felt there wasn't any hope for him accepting Christ – that he just wasn't interested. Oh, how thankful I am God doesn't rely on our prayers to accomplish His will in people's lives. He was with Walt in the lowest places and He spared his life when it was so dismal. Finally Walt did realize his own need for Christ, and he gave his life to Him. Witnessing that was truly a humbling experience for me and my mother.

Now, "Santa's Brother" has his own mission at Christmas. On Christmas Eve, in Hawthorne, Florida, Walt and his wife, Mary, open their home to members of the local alcohol and drug abuse recovery chapters, providing a dinner for anyone who doesn't have a family with which to share the Christmas holidays.

Santa Chooses a Career

I've been interested in art ever since my pre-school days. I remember painstakingly completing a "paint-by-number" pair of elephants for my nursery school teacher. She was so pleased with the gift she had the paintings framed and placed over the mantel in the house on Lindsay Street that was the Toddle Time Nursery School. In elementary school, I became fond of the Jack London adventure stories, and inspired by one of those stories, I even created my own *original* painting on black velvet. The painting hangs in my Santa House today.

As a hobby, my Dad gave "chalk talks" to various civic groups in and around our community. He had developed the ability to draw most of the cartoon characters popular at the time. He had a big board with drawing paper on it, which he made at his print shop. He would place the board on an easel in front of his audience, and then, with a big black crayon, sketch a character while giving an inspirational talk to his listeners. At first the rapid marks he made on the paper didn't seem to make sense, but as his listeners became involved in his story, a character would appear. When he finished his story he would tear the drawing off the easel pad and give it to someone in the audience. If time permitted, he would start another story and drawing.

Young and old alike enjoyed Dad's talks. Unfortunately, they are only a fond memory, as he never saved any of his drawings. Dad always ended his talks by reciting a poem about a smile. I don't remember the entire poem, but the last line was, "A smile is only valuable if you give it away." That's the way my father lived his life, by giving himself away. What a great legacy for Santa Claus.

Since my interest in fine art had continued through college, I did my senior thesis on the Wyeth family of painters who lived in the Brandywine area of Pennsylvania. Apparently that study had left me with the impression of artists living in their own "secret world." To this day, N. C. Wyeth is my favorite artist. I am especially fascinated by the illustrations he created for the literary classics like *Robin Hood, Last of the Mohicans, Ivanhoe* and *Robinson Crusoe.* Perhaps it was because Wyeth actually took on the character of his subjects and dressed himself in the costumes he depicted them in that fascinated me. (Could he have been an inspiration for my career as Santa Claus?)

Perhaps it was this interest in art, inspired by my father's hobby which made me interested in the artist's life. After college, I was too intent on starting a job to even think about pursuing my own artistic interests. Eventually, my career path led me to Hall Printing Company in my hometown of High Point, North Carolina. Bill Hall, Jr. had encouraged me to pursue a graphic-arts education, since he had graduated from Carnegie-Mellon University in Pennsylvania himself. In many ways, he became my second father. As a result, a bond of respect and creativity began between us that lasted for the next twenty-five years. He continued the training in the production of fine printing that my dad had started when I worked by his side.

After beginning my profession in printing sales, I thought it would be interesting to call on an artist who made their living painting original art. The first artist I went to see was Bob Timberlake, who lived in nearby Lexington, North Carolina. At the time, we had just finished printing one of his paintings as a Christmas card for a local insurance company. I was eager to meet the man who had painted such a realistic watercolor of Christ Church, the oldest church still standing in North Carolina. That meeting will be etched in my memory forever, because I truly believe Bob Timberlake changed the course of my life.

It was a cold day in February of 1972 when I knocked on the back door of Bob's house. He used a single room (once a bedroom for his son, who was off in college), as his studio. He immediately shattered my pre-conceived artist's identity. He was a warm, sincere and charismatic man. Before long, we were deep into a discussion about his life as an artist, his involvement in his family businesses, and his family which consisted of three children and his lovely wife, Kay. In fact, after several hours of talking, Kay brought us a plate of cheeseburgers which we enjoyed by the Franklin stove in his studio

Bob had recently made the decision to leave his family business responsibilities so he could devote his full time to painting. He was still conflicted as to whether he could actually support his family as an artist. One of his paintings, "My Yankee Drum," had been reproduced as a limited-edition print by a publisher and had been fairly successful. However, Bob felt, with his business background, he could better market his own work without having to be part of a large stable of artists controlled by a publisher. Being impressed with the job our printing company had done on his Christmas card, he asked if we could reproduce larger-sized paintings into limited-editions. Not being completely sure of my answer, but having complete faith in the craftsmanship of my mentor, Bill Hall, I told him I thought no one could do a better job than we would.

That response seemed to satisfy my new customer and he proceeded to bring out three reproduction examples of his paintings done by other printers. He personalized each one to me and said we could use them as samples for our project and could keep them afterward. I couldn't believe he was actually giving me reproductions that would sell for $75 in an art gallery. He gave me instructions on where to go to borrow the painting he wanted to reproduce titled, "Rowboat." We had not discussed a price, delivery date, or any of the normal business details that would be part of such a meeting; yet I left Bob Timberlake's house with my first limited-edition art reproduction order.

The next week, Bill Hall and I loaded his Suburban with our luggage, tied a canoe to the roof and headed east for Whiteville, which is near the North Carolina coast. We were on a mission. Surely the family who owned "Rowboat" was a little apprehensive about letting one of their prized possessions leave with two strangers, but they did turn it over to us. We carefully wrapped their painting in a quilt and carried it out to his vehicle. I can only imagine the canoe on top of his truck did not add to their confidence, but Bob Timberlake had already assured them their painting would be in good hands.

Well, let me tell you Bill Hall and I felt like we were on top of the world! We had just picked up the item that was to be the beginning of a specialized form of printing which would lead to national recognition for our company. We were so excited we decided to take the rest of the afternoon and do a little fishing in the Lumber River. We spent the rest of the day excitedly talking about how we were going to learn to print limited-edition art reproductions. We didn't catch any fish that day; I guess the "big fish" was already in the car!

Bill Hall and I went on to produce over 100 reproductions of Bob Timberlake's paintings together. In addition to his work, we printed art reproductions for artists from all over the country. These projects consistently won best-of-category awards in printing trade competitions. Every year thereafter, Hall Printing Company was recognized for its quality work, thanks to the master craftsmanship of Bill Hall and his talented staff.

Bob Timberlake has gained national and international acclaim as an artist. He was received in the White House by three different presidents and even had the opportunity to share watercolor painting tips with Prince Charles at Buckingham Palace. After beginning to market his own work, Bob's signed-and-numbered reproductions began to sell out. Soon each edition was pre-subscribed by dealers and collectors across the country, making the secondary market values of those sold-out prints skyrocket. The success of his limited-edition sales helped Bob build The Bob Timberlake Gallery, where he showcases his original art, reproductions, furniture and accessories to thousands of visitors each year.

Not only did Bob Timberlake help determine a career path for me, he opened the public's eyes to the appreciation of fine art in our area. I believe he was the guiding force that has made North Carolina truly a "State of the arts."

"Merry Christmas"

One of the greatest pleasures of knowing Bob Timberlake was also the privilege of knowing his parents, Casper and Ella Timberlake. "Pappy," as he was called by his family and friends, was well-known as a businessman in Davidson County, North Carolina. He owned the local propane gas company as well as the town's funeral home. He had known many of his customers literally "from the cradle to the grave" and was respected by everyone who knew him.

It is easy to see where Bob got his charisma and personality. Pappy Timberlake never met a stranger. He enthusiastically greeted everyone and made them feel like a friend, like their needs were important to him.

The most endearing thing I remember about Pappy was his standard greeting…"Merry Christmas!" In the middle of July, even, his salutation would be the same. He lived his life as if it were Christmas all year. It occurred to me; what a great way to live my life, like it was Christmas every day.

After Bob Timberlake lost his parents (Ella first and then Pappy), I remember visiting him one afternoon and being greeted with "Merry Christmas!" I smiled as I thought of his father and what a wonderful tribute Bob had just paid to his memory.

Over the last several years, there have been those who have sought to remove the words, "Merry Christmas," from our holiday vocabulary. There are even some commercial establishments where Santa visits that instruct him NOT to say "Merry Christmas" to his visitors. Now, whoever heard of Santa Claus not greeting people with a hearty, "Ho, Ho, Ho, M-E-R-R-Y C-H-R-I-S-T-M-A-S!"? I, for one, could never resist saying that. The phrase itself embodies the true meaning of the season, for its root word "Christ" is the whole reason we celebrate the season in the first place.

I think I will adopt the greeting of my friends, Pappy and Bob Timberlake, and of course, Santa Claus. I am going to wish folks a "Merry Christmas" as often as I can, every day of the year!

Santa and the Arts

I have enjoyed finding paintings and drawings of Santa Claus and seeing how different artists have portrayed the famous gift-giver. It would be interesting to know how many different images have been created of him over the ages. I would think they would be second only to images of Jesus Christ.

Most of us now recognize the "Coca-Cola® Santa" images created by artist, Haddon Sundblom (beginning in 1931), as the standard look for an American Santa. It is recorded that Sundblom used his own likeness as a model for many of his Santa Claus paintings. He also used himself as the model for the Quaker Oats character he created.

While Haddon Sundblom was pursuing his art career in Chicago during the 1950s, a young artist named Ralph J. McDonald would occasionally visit the studio of the master painter and watch him work. Young McDonald had recently graduated from art school and was a teacher of life drawing classes at his alma mater. He has since distinguished himself as an internationally-known wildlife artist, and was designated the International Ducks Unlimited Artist of the Year for 2006-07.

While attending the Southeastern Wildlife Festival in Charleston, South Carolina in 1998, I happened to run into Ralph McDonald, who was exhibiting there. I had spoken with the artist a few times before; and we sell his reproductions in the art gallery my wife and I own. When he saw me, he said, "Hey, you would make a good model for my Santa Claus paintings." Since 1990, he has offered an annual limited-edition reproduction of Santa to his collectors. Since I have always been impressed with Ralph's art (especially his Santa images), my head swelled a little at the mere suggestion.

Sure enough, McDonald invited me to his Gallatin, Tennessee home, near Nashville, in July of that same year. I took my entire Santa wardrobe with me; and, in the summer Tennessee heat, he snapped away, photographing Santa in all sorts of situations.

One my favorite features about Ralph's Santa paintings is that he includes reference to the Nativity, in some way, in his compositions. The first painting we collaborated on, "The Christmas Story," was released in 2000. It portrays Santa sitting on a log, in a snowy forest, telling a story to the animals. The *real* Christmas Story (The Nativity) is shadowed in the painting's background. A stint as an illustrator for The Methodist Publishing House, and his own personal faith, gave him perfect knowledge of his subject matter.

For the last several years, two or three artists have painted new images of me, as Santa, each year. To date, nine different artists have chosen to create over twenty-five holiday originals, which have been reproduced on paper and canvas, and some have been made into greeting cards and decorative accessories.

It is flattering to be Santa for all of my artistic friends. I truly believe all of my background and training has brought me to the place I find myself today. In her book, *The Artist's Way*, Julia Cameron emphasizes that God has already given us all of the creativity we need to be the unique individuals He intends us to be. In my heart, I know my role as Santa Claus is a "gift from God." Having my image as Santa in front of people, most of whom I will never be able to meet in person, is an awesome privilege.

"Poppy Claus"

When we found out we were going to be grandparents, my wife and I decided we wanted our future grandchildren to call us "Poppy" and "Nana."

When Carrie Morgan Snider, our first granddaughter was born, our lives changed forever! From the moment we saw her, our hearts were captured; we just knew there could be no greater joy than being a grandparent. I remember calling my daughter-in-law at odd times of the day and asking her if I could stop by just to see Carrie. How wonderful it was to have a little baby to hold in my arms. She became my motivation to pursue my role as Santa Claus with even greater fervor.

When Carrie was about eighteen months old, she saw me dressed as Santa for the first time. I had on my red suit, my new boots and white gloves. My face and head were covered by an artificial wig and beard. She was expectedly stand-offish as I tried my best to assume *the* role. Finally, as I walked away after speaking to her, I heard a small, timid voice call out, "Poppy?" She obviously had not been fooled!

Our second granddaughter, Madeline Noëlle Keefer, was born to our daughter, Carole, and her husband Tommy, in December, 1993, in Kalamazoo, Michigan. She was named after my wife's mother, Madeline, and got her middle name from Carole, which means "song of joy." I think Noëlle is an appropriate name for one of Santa's granddaughters. What a wonderful Christmas present it was to travel to Michigan on Christmas Eve that year to spend the holidays with our daughter and her new family.

"Maddie," as we call her, became a big sister exactly 12 months and 12 days later, right after Christmas. Rachael Caroline Keefer, looked just like our daughter, and to this day, we feel like we are getting to see Carole grow up again. We love the fact that Rachael means "little lamb" and "Caroline" also means "song of joy." We were blessed to be in Michigan for her birth and to spend the New Year with her family.

My son, Robert Clifton Snider III, told his new wife, Laura, that if they had a son, he was going to name him Robert Clifton Snider IV. Laura didn't have any choice in the matter, and sure enough, my namesake was born in 1996. I was one proud "Poppy" to have my first grandson.

1996 was the year I decided to pursue my *formal* education as Santa Claus. When I got my first "professional" Santa suit in 1995, the owner of the Santa Claus Suit and Equipment Company told me about The Charles W. Howard Santa Claus School in Midland, Michigan. He told me the school was the oldest and most respected Santa Claus school in the nation. It was founded in 1937 by Charlie Howard, one of the original Macy's Department Store Santas. I applied to the school and was requested to write an essay about why I wanted to be Santa Claus. The school, at the time, only admitted ten new students per year, so I was thrilled when they accepted my application.

In October, 1996, the dean of the school, Tom Valent, met me at the small Midland airport. My instruction into the world of "Santa-dom" had begun. For the next four days I learned all about how to "be" Santa. I also met some of the finest men and women I have ever had the privilege of knowing, and ironically, many of them looked just like the *real* Santa. I also had the pleasure of meeting Tom's lovely "Mrs. Claus," Holly.

Since Midland is only a few hours away from Kalamazoo, our daughter surprised me by bringing her girls to see me. They spent the night at my motel and Carole drove me to the airport the next day. In the little terminal, I hugged my daughter and then my grand-daughters; Maddie first and then Rachael. Rachael wasn't quite two years old yet. I told her, "I sure do love you, Rachael!" Her response to me was, "I sure do love you too, 'Poppy Claus!'" I had been given a new name, and I liked it!

Our second grandson was born to Carole and Tommy in 1998. My "quote of endearment" from Daniel came when he was about four years old. He was sitting in my lap listening to me read him a story – one of my favorite things to do with any of my grandchildren. He looked up at me for a long time before posing the question, "Poppy, why do you have peanuts in your ears?" Thus was his reaction to my new hearing aids!

Returning from a second visit to the Charles W. Howard School as an alumnus in 1998, I brought home a piece of sheepskin which had been fashioned into a beard with elastic attached to hold it on. While visiting in my son's home for Christmas that year, I showed it to my (then two-year old) grandson, Robby. The next thing we knew, little Robby was standing up on his potty chair in front of the bathroom mirror. He had on the sheepskin beard and was bellowing into the mirror for all he was worth, "Ho, ho, ho, kiddies, Merry Christmas!"

A few years later someone asked my son, Rob, "Are you going to be the next Santa Claus?" His response was, "No, my son has declared that HE is going to be the next Santa Claus."

Having a quiver of five grandchildren, people often ask me what they think about their grandfather portraying such a character. I've never really had to have a discussion with any of them about my identity. This is the only way they have known me. They are the ones who tell their friends that their grandfather is Santa Claus, even the oldest who turned seventeen this year.

After my wife's sister passed away in 2004, we humbly, yet enthusiastically, began grand parenting her grandchildren as well. Andrew David Pardo was six at the time, and his sister Alexandra Nicole, was four. They had never had much contact with "Santa Claus," so they seemed really excited to have *him* as a member of their family. In 2003, their twin cousins, Billy and Abby, were born in New Hampshire. Even though we don't get to physically interact with them the same as we do the other grandchildren, we like to claim the charming five-year-old duo as well.

During my premier appearance at Christmas Castle in 2006, some of my first visitors were Billy, Abby, and their parents, Bill and Holly. They had prepared the children for six months about the trip to see Santa and his castle. They got right into Santa's throne room (where I was), and little Billy would not have a thing to do with me! His sister, however, climbed right up onto my lap for pictures while Billy pouted.

On the way back home Bill and Holly asked Billy what his favorite part of Christmas Castle was, and his reply was, "The Grinch!" Interestingly enough, however, I heard that after Christmas, Billy began telling his little friends in New Hampshire that Santa Claus had moved to a castle in North Carolina. Can you imagine the confusion that fact created for his buddies?

Now, like with any "hobby," it is easy for me to get carried away financially seeking to the best Santa Claus accessories I can afford. Thus, it has become customary for me to "give myself a present" each year on my birthday.

Having seen the awesome belts made by a fellow Santa, Richard Christie, I knew I had to have one. Selecting his "Father Christmas" belt and suspenders with the name

"S.A.N.T.A" beautifully carved into an eight-inch gold buckle, I approached my wife with the idea of ordering the belt. Her response was, "Why do you need a belt with your name on it? Everyone knows you are Santa." That seemed like a reasonable question, so I called Santa Richard (who lives in California), and asked him the same question. He wisely told me that children often need a "hook" to hold their attention, especially if they are shy or afraid of you. If they are just learning their letters, you let them spell out the name that's on your belt and often capture their hearts in the process. His explanation made perfect sense to me, so the belt was ordered.

It is tradition for our family to celebrate each member's birthday with a family dinner. So, on August 7, 2002, we gathered at our house for my birthday. My son, and his family, my wife, my mother and I had just finished dinner when I excused myself. I went to my room and put on my new Father Christmas belt. Rejoining everyone, I proudly asked Robby, who was six years old at the time, what the letters on my belt spelled. He carefully spelled out "S.A.N.T.A." then exclaimed, "SANTA!" His eyes beamed and his toothless smile widened and so did mine as he certified my belt as being worth every penny of its considerable price!

As everyone applauded and laughed together, Robby turned to his mother and asked, "Does that mean he's the *Real One?* Suddenly, like in the credit card commercials on TV, my belt became *priceless*! Come to think about it, that is how I paid for it!

Four Fingers or Five?

As I have grown in my role as Santa Claus, it amazes me just how accurately I can predict the age of most children who visit with me. I can also tell ahead of time which children are going to accept an *interview* with "the man himself," and which ones will be led "kicking and screaming" to Santa's lap. If a young child does agree to sit with me, I usually start the conversation with, "And how old are you?" If the child is younger than three, we usually play the "finger game," where they try to hold up the right number of fingers to indicate their age. It is so much fun to watch their precious little hands working with such effort.

Usually by the time children are four or five years old, they have gotten over their fear of Santa and are prepared to give him all of the information he needs to carry their wishes back to the North Pole.

Occasionally a boy might say, "If you are really Santa, you should already know my name!" I usually play along and confess that, in my old age, I sometimes forget my own name; that's why it's on my belt buckle! We all get a laugh together, and then he will tell me his name.

Being hearing impaired, I always have the children sit on my left knee (the side of my better ear) and carefully concentrate on hearing their names correctly. After all, Santa needs to be sure to get each child's name right. Often I will ask a child to spell his or her name for me and will write it in my "book of good girls and boys." I think having their name in Santa's book is sometimes more important to them than what they want for Christmas.

Years ago, I wore gloves when visiting with children. Some public Santa venues, like malls, require Santa to wear gloves both for his own health, and so his hands can be visible at all times. While I understand the need for such protocol, I feel gloves are impersonal, and, perhaps even too sterile for the intimate conversation taking place between a child and Santa. I wouldn't take anything for the feel of a tiny hand, especially when a child leads me to my chair.

When I was working during my college days in Rochester, New York, the owner of Rochester Book Bindery on Saint Paul Street made a lasting impression on me from the very first day he hired me. To begin with, he was a giant of a man, well over six and a half feet tall and weighed close to four hundred pounds. He had a booming voice, and his laughter would often fill the large, ancient building that housed the business. On the day we met, we shook hands to establish our relationship. That's when I noticed he only had four fingers. A few weeks after starting my job, I met the owner's father, and he too only had four fingers. I made a mental note of this coincidence, but thought it would be rude to inquire about it.

One of my jobs at the bindery was to take the covers off old books we were restoring, and then shave the glue from the bound edge. This was done on a monster of a machine called a guillotine cutter. Even the name of the machine would strike fear in one's heart; because once any stack of paper (or a book in this case), was placed under the clamp, a large blade would descend and cut the paper. To facilitate the speed of production, the two gentlemen I have referred to had devised a way to by-pass the safety features of the machine. Tiny amounts of waste could be cut off and pulled away from the spine of a book being restored with one hand while operating the blade for the next cut with the other hand. Since some of the books we worked on were priceless library volumes from universities and museums, it was important to only remove enough of the old binding to facilitate a new covering, leaving as much of the original volume as possible.

One day, while working on a project, I reached in to pull the waste shavings away after the blade had dropped. The dull blade had not cut the last few pages and the volume pulled away from the clamp. Down the blade fell again, as it had been rigged to do! My instinct was to grab the book, but the blade was faster than I was, cutting the book completely in half at a diagonal... all three hundred pages!

Needless to say, I was devastated by my mistake and feared losing my job. With much shame and embarrassment, (and still shaking from the incident), I took the ruined remains to my employer, ready to accept my punishment. All he did was hold up his right hand and say, "It could have been a lot worse!" Then, with great forgiveness and compassion he said, "I'll take care of it... just try to be more careful next time." That incident obviously made a deep impression on me, or I wouldn't feel it necessary to share it with you.

My story doesn't end here, however. In my professional interactions with Santas from all over the world, I learned of the following tale from a Santa in Norway. In his country, the *real* Santa Claus only has four fingers on each hand! The reason for this is uncertain; perhaps it is from his elfin ancestry. Therefore, Santas in Norway, I am told, wear four-fingered gloves! When I became aware of this little-known fact, my mind raced back to the Rochester Book Bindery and my first employer, Eugene Eckert, a Norwegian-born book binder.

Could he have been?

"Why Are You So Fat?"

We all know children can be brutally honest. They will often speak what is on their mind before their parents have a chance to stop them.

I had the opportunity to visit in the home of some friends in a neighboring town several years ago. Upon arriving, their son, Josh, greeted me and led me to the family room. Once I took a seat, his first question for me was, "Why are you so fat?" His embarrassed parents quickly rushed in from the kitchen to apologize for their son's boldness, but the question was already out there…"like an elephant in the room!"

Frankly, his question made perfect sense, and it is one I have asked myself my entire life. I have always been *heavy, portly, obese,* or *big for my age*…whatever term you would want to use for "fat."

It would be easy to pass off my size to family DNA, but that would probably only be half right. Most of the Sniders were on the heavy side, while the Hunts (my mother's side) were slim.

That doesn't mean I haven't tried to do something about my weight, however. Being active in sports during high school (playing tackle on the football team), helped keep my weight down somewhat.

Like most of us, after I got married and began to enjoy my wife's great cooking, and especially her mother's, the pounds started packing on. (Janie's mother introduced me to home-made biscuits served with real country-churned butter!) Eventually, the scales tipped at well over 300 pounds and it was evident I wouldn't live long without trying to control my weight.

In 1971, my boss and friend, Bill Hall, challenged me to lose some weight. I joined the local Weight Watchers class and became very dedicated to their wonderful program. Eventually (over a period of about eighteen months), I lost over 100 pounds, reaching my goal weight and becoming a lifetime member. I actually worked as a lecturer for the organization, with classes in two nearby cities. Since there were more than one hundred members in each of those classes, my wife traveled with me each week, and worked as my head clerk. We would even take our children with us sometimes if we couldn't find a baby-sitter. Being a successful male in the mostly women's program, I became sort of a celebrity in the local Weight Watchers circuit, often guest lecturing for other leaders

Unfortunately, like many dieters, my lifestyle hadn't changed; I just concentrated on food intake. Slowly but surely, the pounds began to return, so much so I had to give up my part-time job as a lecturer. It wasn't long until all the pounds had returned.

Like most "yo-yo dieters," I decided to try another program in the 1980s. By following a very strict, medically-supervised diet and eating proprietary foods, I once again lost over 100 pounds. Unfortunately, this time I didn't feel very healthy, I just looked thin. Maintaining the low weight proved to be impossible for me and, again, over the next few years the pounds began to return.

The 1990s found me battling the bulge again, along with a host of other obesity-related problems, including high blood pressure and arthritis. Then in 1998, my doctors discovered my left hip was fractured and had to be replaced. The surgeon was concerned I was too heavy to undergo surgery, and suggested I lose as much weight possible. He also encouraged me to exercise my muscles and joints so my post-operative recovery would be easier.

The word "exercise" had not been part of my vocabulary for over thirty years! It turns out that was the ingredient missing from all the previous diets I had attempted. I took to exercise "like a duck takes to water." In fact, water exercise was the only type of activity I could do at first because it didn't do more damage to my joints.

Since the local YWCA is close to my home, and the pool there is really nice, I actually looked forward to swimming laps. After all, I had been a good swimmer in my Boy Scout days; it should be fun. However, my first attempt at laps after such a long hiatus did not go well. I thought I would drown before reaching the other end of the pool! Boy, it really hurt to realize what bad shape I was in. Eventually, by sheer determination and perseverance, I could swim a mile in less than an hour. In the process, more than twenty-five pounds had disappeared, so hip-replacement surgery was scheduled for that summer.

The fear of not being able to properly walk again sent me right back to the pool after my medically-supervised physical therapy. I had finally learned the only way to maintain anywhere close to a healthy weight and feeling of wellness is through diet AND exercise.

Occasionally I will hear comments, (usually from adults) like, "Looking a little skinny there, Santa," or "Hasn't Mrs. Claus been feeding you lately?" I tell them Santa has decided if he wants to continue his long life, he needs to take better care of himself. I even have to remind myself of the same thing from time to time.

I now like to refer to myself as "the Santa of the New Millennium"…a healthier version of the Santa we have all known in the past.

Santa's Bracelet

As far back as I can remember, I always wanted to have a daughter when I became a husband. Growing up with only a brother to relate to as a sibling, I wondered what it would be like to have a girl around the house. Years later, my wife and I dreamed about buying cute outfits for a baby girl, and about her becoming "Daddy's little girl."

Those dreams came true when our daughter, Eva Carole, was born during my college years. Her arrival set me on a path toward maturity at a very young age. I suddenly realized there was a new person in this world who was totally dependent on her mother first, and then me, for her support and well-being.

Carole was born just a few hours after we arrived at the hospital. When the nurse came to the lobby and informed me that I was the father of a little girl, I was beside myself with excitement. She told me it would be a little while before I could see my wife and baby, so I excitedly phoned home with the "good news." After what seemed like forever, I was taken to the hospital recovery room where Janie and our daughter were enjoying seeing each other for the first time. I picked up the little pink bundle and checked her over from head to toe... (she has my toes). I fell in love with her immediately, never thinking about whether or not that love would be reciprocated.

The years flew by as Carole grew into quite a beautiful young lady, both inside and out. Knowing that we couldn't afford full tuition and other expenses at most colleges, we told her we would match, dollar for dollar, what she invested in her own education. It could come from scholarship money, savings, gifts or part-time jobs. Carole accepted the challenge and was awarded two scholarships; one in music and one for academics, to Appalachian State University. She quickly applied all her efforts undertaking a strenuous double-major curriculum in performance keyboard and cello. In addition to her scholarship funds, she took part-time job assignments at school as well as working summers and holidays back at home

Even though Carole had worked and made her own spending money, I wasn't prepared for the gift she gave me for Christmas one year. It was a beautiful gold bracelet. I was overwhelmed with the gift, and put it on my right arm immediately. She seemed pleased to be the giver of such a special gift, and I was certainly thrilled to be the receiver. I wear Carole's bracelet every day, and when I put it on I think fondly of "Daddy's little girl."

Later the truth was revealed that Carole had found the bracelet in the snow beneath her campus apartment mailbox. She had turned it in to the lost and found office, and when no one claimed it, she was allowed to keep it. After having it cleaned, she presented the gift to her new boyfriend with excitement. It turned out the bracelet was too big for him, and since he wasn't really "into" jewelry, Daddy was her second choice! I really didn't mind though, because I have the bracelet to remind me of how precious she is to me.

A Gift for Santa

Of course everyone comes to Santa to make their requests for Christmas. Since he is known for bringing gifts to good boys and girls, it is rare that anyone brings a gift for Santa himself.

One of my first engagements as a professional Santa was for a craft fair held at a vacant shopping center in my hometown. The empty stores and large common areas made it an excellent place to hold the event. Sponsored by our local newspaper, *The High Point Enterprise*, the holiday show featured vendors from the surrounding areas as well as out-of-state crafters.

Most of my Santa appearances prior to this time had been for family and friends; I had not had very many encounters with the general public. We allowed guests to take their own photographs, so everyone felt free to approach Santa. Of course I experienced the same range of reactions, from complete delight to sheer terror, from my visitors that any Santa usually encounters.

My day passed quickly and I really enjoyed interacting with everyone. Since I had lived in my hometown most of my life, it was not unusual for me to call out to people by their name, much to their surprise and delight. Of course when I did, they always wanted to know who I was; and sometimes it was difficult to convince them my name was "Santa Claus!" I have since had a driver's license made for my Santa identification. It always makes a believer out of the most hardened skeptics, especially teenagers. To them a driver's license is a "rite of passage" which really proves who you are. Of course they seldom take time to read the "fine print" defining DMV as "Department of Many Visits!"

During the first morning of the three-day event, I noticed a young lady standing off to the side watching everything going on. I say she was a young lady because she appeared to be 16 or 17 years old and was as large as an adult. She was dressed in a bright red sweat suit and appeared to have Down syndrome. She would not approach Santa, but would just smile a wonderful, heart-warming smile and wave to me from a distance. Finally, after everyone else had left, I asked her, "Don't you want to come and visit with Santa?" Reluctantly and slowly, she approached me. I held out my hand to her and asked if she wanted to sit on my lap. She seemed embarrassed at first but eventually sat on my left knee and we began to have a pleasant conversation.

Dolly was from Louisiana and she was, in fact, seventeen years old. Her parents made their living traveling from town to town selling their crafts at weekend fairs and festivals. She traveled with them in their motor home where they could care for her needs and home-school her. She was quite intelligent, although at times it was difficult to understand what she was trying to convey. We discussed many things and learned we both enjoyed music when I told her Santa enjoys playing the violin.

As people began to gather again, Dolly told me she needed to get back to help in her parents' booth. I thanked her for our nice visit, gave her a big hug and a candy cane and invited her to come back to see me any time she wanted. After saying our "goodbyes," she sheepishly slipped by the other children waiting at the Santa set. I quickly became busy with my next guest and the day moved on.

After lunch, I returned to my place and began afternoon visits with the children. Soon, Dolly appeared on the outskirts of the area again and began smiling at me when our eyes would meet. She patiently waited until the crowd cleared, then came right up and sat down gently on my knee. We continued our conversation right where we had left off. While we talked about music and art, I asked her if she enjoyed traveling around the country with her family. The time passed quickly and before long she became restless as she realized people were waiting to see Santa. She departed with another candy cane.

This routine continued throughout the entire weekend. Dolly would watch the crowd around Santa disperse and then come up for her turn, always with a warm smile and an equally warm greeting for me. By the end of the show, we must have visited seven different times.

On the last day of the fair, Dolly's parents came by and thanked me for spending time with their daughter, and for being so kind to her. I assured them Dolly had been a joy to be around and was sure they felt the same way. They asked if I could stop by their craft booth before leaving so Dolly could tell me "goodbye." After gathering myself together, I went by to see Dolly and her family. Their craft specialty was ceramic-ware figurines including many Santas. I was admiring the work when Dolly handed me a package wrapped in tissue paper. It held a beautiful, white "Cajun Santa" in a long robe, playing a fiddle! Dolly's reply to my delight was, "This is a gift for you, Santa, from your new friend from Louisiana." Tears came to my eyes as I thanked her and told her how rare it is for anyone to give Santa a gift.

Today, "Dolly's Santa" is one of my prized possessions among my growing collection of Santa figurines. Every time I see it I think of her kindness and her beautiful smile that lit up the room. With all the limitations her condition had placed on her life, her warm and gentle spirit shined through and made me a specially-blessed Santa Claus.

Santa's Book

Santa Claus knows he can't really promise anything to the children who visit him. After all, he needs to check his inventory at the North Pole, confer with his elves to see if they have certain items, and of course he has to check his "naughty or nice" book.

Having been Santa for several years, I have decided there really shouldn't be a "naughty or nice" list. I believe in my heart that, to Santa, all children (especially those who still believe in him) belong on the *nice* list. For that reason I carry a little red book in which I often write the names of children who visit me, along with their Christmas request.

Over the years, the list of names in my "Santa's Book" has grown. I can even go back through the pages and remind my regular visitors about their requests from previous years. It really surprises them when I ask if they enjoyed the Barbie doll or fire truck or bicycle they received the year before.

Also, since my book has become filled with different names, I can usually find any name I am looking for, so it becomes a valuable "ice-breaker." Often a child will want to know if his or her name is in Santa's Book, so together we will begin looking. After intently searching, their eyes light up upon finding it. If after a few pages we don't find it, I just tell them I will have to write it in. Then, with pen in hand, I have him or her tell me what his or her name is, the spelling, and a Christmas wish. I can see and feel the sense of security it gives children to know their names are in Santa's Book.

During one special visit with some children, a young boy, who appeared to be about seven years old, hung to the back of the line, apparently hoping for a private audience with Santa Claus. After he climbed onto my lap, we exchanged the usual greetings and I asked him what he would like for Christmas. I was surprised when he said, "Nothing;" then he pulled me to him preparing to whisper in my ear.

Once close enough for him to be sure no one else would hear his request, he told me, "All I want for Christmas is for the children in my school to quit picking on me and calling me names." My heart instantly broke, as I remembered feeling the same way when I was his age. I felt even worse realizing that he believed Santa could change his circumstances. There was no way I could keep the children from making fun of him – that was a promise Santa could not make.

Suddenly, realizing that my "Santa's Book" was in my suit coat, I said, "I understand how you feel, son, but Santa can't make children be kind to one another. I will promise to write your name in my book and say my prayers for you before going to bed tonight." A warm smile came over the young man's face as he meekly replied, "O K." That was all he had to tell me, so I gave him a big hug and he was on his way.

Just as he left my lap, I sensed an inner voice speaking to me, "That is a promise you *can* keep, Santa!" So that night, after a long day's work, I took out my Santa's Book, turned to the page with the boy's name on it, and began talking to God about his request. As I prayed, it seemed as if heaven opened up and every angel heard my petition. I knew in my heart my prayer for this boy was being heard.

Many names and circumstances have been added to what I now call "Santa's Prayer Book." The book still delights children of all ages when we search the pages for their names. Many remember the book and ask if they can see it. It stays in a designated pocket in the hem of my coat. Each name and request is important and represents a special visit with young and old alike. But the greatest significance is the privilege I have to "keep Santa's promise" to pray for the individual names and requests hidden in its pages. I now realize that when I pray for those children, I may be the only person who has ever lifted their name to heaven.

What an awesome privilege Santa has to represent such precious children and what confidence I now have that there IS one promise this Santa can keep!

"...And Nuts and Fruit and Candy!"

That is the way I always ended my visit with Santa Claus when I was a young lad. Nuts and fruits and candy were as important to me at Christmas as presents were, maybe even more important! My family wasn't poor, but my parents had to work hard for a living, and nuts and fruits were luxuries reserved only for Christmas, and especially candy—hard candy.

When I was about five or six years old, my mother hand knitted a Christmas stocking for my brother, Walt, and me. Actually Walt couldn't pronounce my name, so he called me "Kicky" and I called him "Lumpy." We still call each other by those names today; although he has recently changed my name to "Kicky Claus." Each year, as we began our decorating for the Christmas holiday, our stockings were always hung "by the chimney with care." The anticipation of what might fill those stockings caused as much excitement in my brother and me as wondering what Santa would leave under our family Christmas tree.

And Santa ALWAYS delivered!

Every Christmas morning my stocking would have almost doubled in size, bulging at the seams as it strained to stay on its mantel hook. After the excitement of seeing what Santa had left us under the tree and opening one gift apiece from Mom and Dad, my brother and I would take our stockings down to see what treats were hidden inside.

There was always a cellophane-wrapped candy cane sticking out of the top from Santa, right next to a bright red-delicious apple. There would be chocolate-covered bon-

bons, gum drops, hard stick-candy in lemon, peppermint and horehound flavors. There would also be a "Story-Book" box of rolled Life Savers with assorted flavors inside. My favorite flavors were wild cherry, butterscotch and wintergreen. I could make those lifesavers last until July if I was careful! I even had a special place in my room where I would hide them for future savoring.

But the most exciting part of the contents of the stocking for me was the nuts – real nuts in the shell! There would be pecans, walnuts, almonds and filberts. The anticipation of enjoying this yearly delicacy was almost more than I could stand. We had a nut-cracking set which had a wooden bowl for the nuts with a section in the middle to hold the tools necessary for breaking open the morsels. My father would ceremoniously bring out the set, crack the nuts, and then give them to us, one at a time, along with a silver pick to pry out the flavorful meat. Then for nearly an hour, we would all have a feast.

Always, in the toe of our stocking would be a FLORIDA orange, or if we were really fortunate, a tangerine. I emphasize they came from Florida because that is where I thought ALL *real* fruit came from. My grandparents spent the winters in Florida, and somehow Santa was able to get whole oranges for our stockings. I really don't remember having fresh fruit any other time of the year.

Of course there were other treats in our stockings, like a new pencil with an attachable rubber eraser for our school work, or a wooden ruler or a pencil box. Sometimes there would be games like Jack Rocks, Fiddle Stix, marbles, or a package of plastic army men.

After opening my stocking full of gifts from Santa, a feeling of contentment would come over me.

As I grew older, my stocking became a "rite of passage" into my teenage years. I got my first container of deodorant in my stocking, as well as my first razor, mug of shaving soap and a brush to lather it on with. It seemed as though Santa knew just what I needed.

I still have the stocking my mother made for me....it hangs right next to the one she made for my wife when we got married over forty-two years ago.

Incidentally, my mother still knits those Christmas stockings. She has made one for each of our children, their spouses, and all of her great-grandchildren. Turning 90 years old in November, Mom now teaches other ladies the fine art of knitting and crocheting, so her skills will be passed on to the next generation. I am sure that before long, she will be knitting Christmas stockings for all of her great-great grandchildren too.

There is only one problem I can see with our tradition of Christmas stockings. As Santa Claus, I can't remember the last time a child asked me for "nuts and fruits and candy!" These things are such a normal part of every child's diet these days that they no longer represent a special Christmas treat.

That makes me sad.

Santa's Sister

One of the advantages, or disadvantages, in being a real-bearded Santa Claus is appearing older than you really are. To the children and adults you visit with each year, it makes you appear to be wiser, like Santa should be, and that is a good thing. However, for the person you share your life with (your wife), it can be a bad thing if she looks younger than you do.

I had a beard and mustache for twenty years or so before deciding to let it all grow to become more authentic as Santa Claus. In 1995 I put away my razor and haven't used one since. While trying to keep my beard neat so it doesn't look too "wild," I will let it grow to a fairly long length and then trim a little off occasionally to keep it healthy.

Once my beard grew longer, it had a nice shape but there was one problem. It was all colors…brown, red, gray, and white; but not pure white like Santa's beard should be. The only way to achieve having white hair was to bleach my natural color out. Looking for a beautician who would do such a job for me was not an easy task. No one wanted to take on the chance of damaging my hair, even possibly causing it to fall out. Finally, I found a lady who bleached her own hair, and she felt comfortable enough accepting the challenge to do the job properly.

My first visit to her salon was quite an ordeal! For almost three hours she applied bleach to my roots first and then to the longer strands of hair. Once that was completed, she covered my head with plastic, prompting body heat to activate the bleaching process. The fumes were so bad I had to breathe through a straw and put cotton balls in my nostrils! If a child had seen me in that condition, they would have been terrified. The bleach would burn wherever it came in contact with my skin, and I remember thinking to myself, "What have I done? I wonder how long I will have to do this before my hair turns naturally white." However, after she had finished the washing, blow-drying and setting, the result was a beautiful, authentic-looking Santa Claus.

The first year I had the bleaching done it was sometime around Halloween. I remember two of my grandchildren seeing me right after the ordeal, and they exclaimed, "Poppy, what happened to your hair?" My reply to them was then, and ever since, has been, "Oh, Poppy's hair turns white with the first frost." It made sense to them that the onset of cold weather could turn Santa's beard white like snow. After all, it does happen around the same "first frost" time every year.

My wife's comments, on the other hand, were quite different. She told me I aged twenty years in one afternoon! She felt like she was married to a strange, older man. When we go out to dinner, often we are with my mother, who has beautiful white hair. Since my mother is 89 years old and needs assistance, I help her to the car when we go places. I've often overheard people make comments like, "What a cute little couple."

Last year my wife and I were attending a Bible study and, as we were saying goodbye to the other participants, one lady asked me, "How is your sister doing?" I replied, "My sister?" She said "Yes, the sweet little lady in our knitting class." Taken aback, I revealed, "She's not my sister, she's my mother!" Once and for all, I realized I had stepped over that imaginary line − I look like an old person! I was ready to go home and find my razor! And all my loving wife could say, between her laughter was, "See, I told you so!"

I've given that night's incident a lot of thought since then. It's true the white hair and beard make me look older than my 61 years, but I like to think with them has come wisdom and a mellowness of spirit befitting Santa Claus. Our children are grown now with children of their own. My bride of forty-two years is by my side as my sweetheart, companion and best friend; and I am fortunate to have my mother (i.e. "my sister").

I truly am a blessed man.

Santa's House

Have you ever wondered what Santa's house looks like? I can just imagine how it must be. Part of the fun I have as Santa Claus has evolved as I have tried to create my own interpretation of Santa's house.

It all started innocently enough when I began collecting Santa Claus memorabilia because of my admiration of the gift-giver from the North Pole. Then, a number of artists began asking me to pose for paintings they wished to create of Santa Claus. Of course, being an art dealer and collector myself, I wanted examples of those paintings and even purchased some of the originals. Many friends, family members and even business associates have also given me Santa figurines – some of which are very impressive, and large!

Before long my collection was in every room of our house and my wife finally put her foot down. Her response to my growing collection was, "I want the celebration of Christmas in our home to be about the birth of Jesus, and not about Santa Claus." She really put me in my place! I am the first to agree with her that Christmas is about the birth of our Savior. In that light, I truly believe being Santa Claus is my calling – to honor Christ by sharing His birth and life with others. But somehow, in my wife's eyes, I had let the *gift-giver* replace the "Giver of Life!" I had to do something.

So that is how my Santa Claus House came to be. You see, we have a garage apartment behind our home that has been used over the years for several purposes. We have leased it to tenants, which was more responsibility than we liked. We used it for a number of years as an office for our publishing company and later as a frame shop for our art gallery. When our son and first granddaughter, Carrie, needed a place to live, it became their home. What better place to house my Santa collection than the place our family affectionately call "The Little House"?

The Little House is a gem in itself. It was built some time during the 1940's as an addition to our home (which was built by an architect in 1927). Made of brick and framing, it is two stories and has about 950 square feet. A small kitchen, dining area, and a living room are on the first floor and two bedrooms and a bath are upstairs. All of the interior walls, cabinets and shelves downstairs are made of beautiful knotty pine which was popular in the 1940s. The living room has a rounded corner fireplace faced with fieldstone native to North Carolina.

Of course Santa's house needs a Christmas tree up all year long! On the tree I was able to hang most of the Christmas ornaments collected over the years. On the mantel over .the fireplace hang nine stockings, one for each of our grandchildren − Carrie, Robby, Maddie, Rachael and Daniel − and one for each of our *adopted* grand-children, Drew, Allie, Billy and Abby. All around the room, on every shelf, are Santa Claus dolls and figurines. On the walls hang the paintings of Santa created by my friends.

Finally, the Christmas tree couldn't hold any more ornaments, so a second, identical tree was selected for the other side of the fireplace. Now when I turn on the light switch in the living room, both trees immediately come to life; lights glow, animated ornaments move, and musical ones play Christmas music. Even the paintings become illuminated. The whole room takes on a feeling of magic.

Every respectful Santa must have a desk where he can take care of paperwork (*or work on lists*). Mine was inherited from my mother, who inherited it from her parents, who inherited it from their parents. It is my understanding the desk is over 150 years old and was used by my great-grandfather, Dr. Harry S. White, who was a professor of calligraphy and penmanship at a business school in Harrisburg, Pennsylvania. What an appropriate provenance for Santa's personal desk. I treasure this heirloom; a diminutive drop-front desk made of beautifully-aged cherry wood. The drawers have cut-glass pulls and some have secret compartments behind them. Inside the desk are Santa's correspondence tools – a goose-quill pen, stationery and a pottery inkwell.

Other furnishings in Santa's House are heirloom antiques as well. A red-velvet Victorian love seat and chair fit quite well, giving more ambiance to the fantasy setting.

So now, in my mind and heart, my "little house" must look just like Santa's House. My next project is to hang Christmas lights on the outside and turn them on at various times of the year (not just at Christmas).

Even though I've given you a complete description of my little "Santa's House," there's more to the big picture. A few years ago, frustrated with not having enough time to decorate our house for Christmas, I bought a large, pre-lit Christmas tree on sale. I took the *two* boxes home and put them in the living room of the "big house." There those boxes sat until one day in October the next year, when our "adopted" grandchildren were visiting. Since they were looking for something to do while waiting for their parents and my wife to return, I suggested we put up the Christmas tree. With great excitement, we began unpacking the boxes. The three of us worked all day putting the sections together and hanging the ornaments before time to place the angel atop the tree. That's when I realized we needed the taller ladder. Our Christmas tree stood well over twelve feet tall! It's a good thing we have a twenty-foot ceiling in that room.

Apprehensive about what my wife's reaction would be, we anxiously waited…but first, we turned on the tree lights. We were so excited we could hardly stand it. When she came in, she actually exclaimed, "It's beautiful!" My instant reply was, "Good, because it's not coming down!

Three years ago, when most of my collection had been moved into its new home, we bought a large Nativity set made of sandstone and arranged it on our hearth in the living room of the "big house." It stays there year round (along with the twelve-foot tree) to remind us of the real meaning of Christmas. Over the mantel is a large painting of "Noah's Ark" reminding us of God's mercy when He gave mankind another chance through the obedience of Noah.

Yesterday was Memorial Day. Seven of our grandchildren spent the weekend with us and I thought it was a great time to turn on the Christmas tree lights. After all, it was a holiday! Turning the tree lights on, I noticed all of the hand-made ornaments collected from our children and grandchildren over the years. The Nativity set was on our hearth and the painting of "Noah's Ark" over the fireplace. I entered the dining room and sat down to say grace with my family. How appropriate it was to thank God, on Memorial Day, for the men and women who gave their lives defending the freedom we have to celebrate Christmas all year long if we want to.

Yes, I know the *Real* Meaning of Christmas, and as for me and my household, we will celebrate it year round.

Reflecting on 9/11

12/29/01

Dear Diary, I don't know how to begin to relate the Santa Season of this year.

A terrible tragedy struck our nation on 9/11/01 when terrorists forced two planes to crash into the towers of the World Trade Center in New York City. The ensuing collapse of the buildings left over 3,000 people dead or missing. Many of the dead were firefighters and policemen who rushed into the buildings attempting to rescue as many people as possible.

At precisely the same time, a third plane crashed into the Pentagon building in Washington, D. C. Over 85 people at the Pentagon died, as well as all the people in the airplane. In addition, a fourth plane crashed in a rural area of Pennsylvania. In order to keep the terrorist hijackers from carrying out their plan, heroic passengers forced the plane down, tragically, at the expense of their own lives and those of their fellow passengers.

All the other events and the war in Iraq, which began as a result of the attack, will certainly be chronicled in future history books. Every American's life changed forever on September 11, 2001.

The weeks following that tragic day found everyone in a state of shock. Many people were afraid other attacks would occur because there were actual, reported threats of such. Air travel was halted for over a week, leaving many apprehensive to get on a plane. I found myself reluctant to travel and cancelled our plans to spend Christmas with our daughter and her family in Michigan.

I imagine many individuals took time to re-evaluate their life and priorities after the attack on America. It made me realize how quickly life could end. It also made me realize how important it is to express the love you have for your family, your Lord, and your country in every way possible every chance that you get.

The events of 9/11 made me more resolved to take my Santa Claus ministry even more seriously, and not be ashamed to speak out as a witness for Christ, especially when talking with children.

Many people began to show various expressions of patriotism in support of our country with flags, banners and other items. Even though production of these patriotic symbols had increased you couldn't even find an American flag in stores for months afterward.

In December, 1863, during the Civil War, a cartoon of Santa Claus passing out gifts to soldiers and children appeared on the front page of *Harper's Weekly* newspaper. The artist was 22-year-old Thomas Nast. He depicted Santa wearing striped-knicker pants, a dark fur-trimmed jacket full of large stars, and a tasseled hat. Remembering that drawing, I contacted a seamstress friend (who had made several outfits for me) and showed her his rendition. We discussed the possibility of her making a similar suit for me.

The 2001 High Point Christmas Parade spectators were the first to see Santa's patriotic statement. The night of the parade was made to order, with the temperature around 30 degrees, a clear sky, and the moon and stars shining brightly. The sight of my new red and white pants, dark blue jacket with large white stars and fur trim seemed to energize the crowd more than usual. Deafening cheers, whistles and applause broke out every time I stood and waved. During the whole evening, no one could have enjoyed themselves more than I did.

Santa Visits America's Largest Home

One of my greatest privileges is being able to work with the talented artists who draw or paint my portrait as Santa Claus. All of these artists have become good friends, and we enjoy combining our individual talents into unique representations of Santa's life.

One of these artists, Teresa Pennington, creates detailed works of art in colored pencil. She is from Waynesville, North Carolina, and is an official artist for the Biltmore Estate and Gardens, located nearby in Asheville. "America's largest home" was built in 1895 by a 33-year-old industrialist named George Washington Vanderbilt, as a retreat from his New York residence. The story of the design and construction of this 250-room mansion in the mountains of North Carolina is remarkable. Vanderbilt even built his own railroad into the estate to transport the tons of granite and lumber used to build the structure.

Hundreds of workers were employed; from landscapers to stone masons to carpenters for a period of more than six years, before the Vanderbilt family moved into their new home. The entire *city* of workers, all in the service of one family, must have rivaled the number of elves in Santa's workshop at the North Pole!

Since the Vanderbilt's first overnight stay at their retreat was on Christmas Eve, 1895, Ms. Pennington and I had many discussions as to how she might depict Santa's visit there. Old photographs showed the mansion decorated for Christmas with lots of beautiful live trees, cut from the forests on the 125,000 acre estate. No doubt the trees were

Frazier Firs, which the area was known for. (As a matter of fact, North Carolina is still known as one of the largest growers of Christmas trees.) Documents revealed that the Vanderbilt home has 65 fire places – all with chimneys – through which Santa could have entered. Now, how in the world could he have picked just one?

One of the most impressive rooms in the estate is the library. With beautiful hand-carved walnut walls and a hand-painted mural on the ceiling, the library contains more than 10,000 leather-bound volumes. The focal point of the room is a magnificent black-marble fireplace, large enough for a grown man to stand upright in it. The pair of bronze andirons inside the fireplace is as big as I am! Ms. Pennington and I decided the library would be Santa's favorite place to visit while at the Vanderbilt mansion; perhaps even taking the time to read the Vanderbilt children a story. So, the scene was set for "A Vanderbilt Christmas." Our next challenge was to stage the necessary photography for the artist to use in her creation.

Permission had to be granted from the Biltmore House Historical Foundation for Ms. Pennington to even render a drawing of their property. Once that was done, we had to demonstrate our ability to create a Santa Claus who would be historically accurate to the period of the estate – right down to the color of his suit. Therefore, a more Victorian-clad Santa was required for the scene. I chose my burgundy-red velvet suit with drop-front knicker pants, green knee-high stockings and square-buckled, period shoes. The fur-trimmed jacket and matching vest have reindeer-stamped antique pewter buttons. Underneath the vest I wore a "puffy" white shirt with ruffles.

The day we arrived on the grounds of the estate, the area where we proposed to have Santa sitting by the fireplace was roped off from access (standard procedure because of public tours). So, a plastic runner was placed over the carpet and a *regular* chair was put in place for me to sit on.

A startling moment occurred when the huge fireplace was lit for our photograph. Having been updated with giant, gas logs, the fire sounded like a freight train coming down the chimney. The roaring blaze was magnificent, and quickly became very hot! There was no way Santa could enter through *that* fireplace if a fire was burning! Before long the heat was more than I could bear, so I removed my coat. Instantly the artist, photographer, and I all agreed we had found our scene. Santa would be sitting by the fire in his vest and shirt, with his coat on the back of the chair. The addition of the Vanderbilt children would have to come from the artist's imagination.

Each year Ms. Pennington is invited to display and sell her artwork on the estate grounds at Christmas. That year we premiered "A Vanderbilt Christmas" (including limited-edition reproductions) at the Carriage House Gift Shop. The weather for the outdoor exhibition that weekend was made to order for Santa Claus. A light snow was falling as I arrived on the scene wearing my Victorian suit, accessorized by a long green "Father Christmas" cloak. Carrying a miner's oil lamp, and a long staff with flowing satin ribbons, my vintage Santa look was complete. Watching people's reactions when they saw me was great fun. I've never seen so many different types of cameras.

While I was there, Ms. Pennington had arranged for my wife and me to have a guided candlelight tour of the estate, which was decorated for Christmas. What a treat it was for me to walk through the beautiful rooms, appearing just as they did when the Vanderbilt family lived there. I felt as though we had truly stepped back in time as we relished the sights and sounds of Christmas in "America's grandest home." I couldn't help but think to myself, "Surely Santa Claus would have been a welcome guest here."

Come As a Child

I'm always thrilled, as Santa Claus, when children eagerly run up to me and jump into my lap. I can usually tell if they are truly excited about their visit with me. There is a twinkle in the eyes of a true "believer" that I think only Santa Claus recognizes. Once a child's eyes meet mine, our hearts are in instant communication. At that moment, as he (or she) enthusiastically rambles off requests, my heart just swells with love for them.

The wonderment of childhood is a precious thing. It's too bad we have to grow up! One of my favorite authors, Julia Cameron, suggests we should discover the child that lives within each of us. She encourages us to act like a child and think like a child. I know in the Bible it says to "put away childish things" as we get older, but I think sometimes some of us forget where we put them!

I have seen the wonderment of childhood in older people as well. One of my first assignments as a professional Santa Claus was at the very church where I was chosen to be Santa when only 15 years old. Wesley Memorial United Methodist Church has an annual Christmas bazaar and they invited me to attend and visit with their guests. I had several conversations with the lady in charge of the event, but had not met her until the first day of the weekend. I arrived early and found my place on the stage in the fellowship hall. There was a comfortable chair for Santa right next to a fireplace with an artificial fire and a beautifully decorated Christmas tree. I had just gotten settled when my hostess arrived to greet me in person. As she walked toward me, she began to cry, and by the time she reached me she was sobbing almost uncontrollably. Somewhat surprised, I asked her what was wrong? She told me that seeing me made her feel just like a child again and that my appearance embodied everything she dreamed the real Santa would look like. Wow! What a compliment!

Another similar incident occurred at an annual Christmas party for my wife's family. Being one of six girls, Janie had quite an extended family of aunts, uncles, cousins and grandchildren. It took the fellowship hall at her parents' church to hold all of us. During one of our parties, I excused myself from the usual covered-dish lunch and retreated to the basement where I changed into a rented Santa Claus costume. After putting on the red suit and adjusting the artificial wig and beard, I returned to the party with a sack full of presents thrown over my shoulder.

Upon entering the room, my wife's oldest aunt, Otelia Whitaker, came right over to me. "Aunt Tillie," as we called her, had Alzheimer's disease and usually didn't know what day it was, or even who she was; but she knew who Santa Claus was, and she wanted to sit in his lap! She plopped all of her 95 pounds on my lap and put her arms around my neck and said sweetly, "Hi Santa; I love you Santa!" A childlike "twinkle" was in her eyes: tears rolled down my cheek. It was a moment I will treasure forever, and the last encounter we had together in her lifetime.

One last "childlike" story comes to my mind. We had been friends with a couple in our church for a number of years. At first, we weren't close, but at a Lay Witness Renewal weekend one year in the 1970s, we got to know each other a little better. As time went by, our lives took us in different directions. We didn't see each other as often as we once had, but whenever we did, we were always delighted to renew our fellowship.

One year while vacationing at the coast, we ran into our friends at a Christmas store. They were aware of my passion for Santa Claus and were amused to see us there. We visited for just a few brief moments and before departing, the husband gave my wife and me a great big hug. We both shared, after they left, how perplexed we were because it was unusual for our friend to be that demonstrative. We later learned he had been diagnosed with cancer and he was giving us a "goodbye" hug. I had the opportunity to fellowship with him several times after that incident, and I treasure the closeness I felt toward him because of that hug.

A few months after our friend passed away, I received a call from his wife asking if Santa could visit her Sunday school class Christmas party. Though surprised she was interested in having me come to her party, I eagerly accepted her invitation. During the festivities Santa selected presents from under the tree and asked each guest to come and receive his or her gift. I then asked each person what he or she would like for Christmas, and we would all have fun as I responded to their requests.

When it was my friend's turn, I asked her the same question. She put her arm around my neck and leaned to whisper in my ear, "Santa, all I want for Christmas is to have my husband back." We both knew her wish could not be granted. To her, Santa Claus was someone who would listen to her request, would not make her feel foolish, and would understand her heartache. In a way, she became just like a little child.

Faith, Hope and Love

Among the wonderful experiences I enjoy upon returning to a Santa Claus school is the opportunity to meet Santas from other countries. I have met Santas from Sweden, Norway, Australia, Germany and Canada.

In 1998, at the Charles W. Howard Santa School, the students were honored with a presentation by a Santa from Sweden and his helper, "Black Peter." Both men were dressed in monk-style attire; Santa was wearing a hooded red robe with white fur trim, and Black Peter a brown robe with a black cord belt. Both men were slim and very austere, with almost a stern countenance.

The pair of characters silently acknowledged each of us as they moved about the room. Santa would give an approving nod or gesture toward certain onlookers, while Black Peter, who was smaller in stature (almost elfin), nervously hid behind Santa and jumped out from time to time, brandishing a switch from his burlap sack. It became quite evident, from the developing drama, that Santa was there to acknowledge the good children, and his counterpart was intent upon punishing the bad. In a room full of adults, the whole scene created a hush of expectation and mystery. Played out in a room full of children, however, I could only imagine the scenario causing a pervading sense of awe, fear and, perhaps, even terror.

The Swedish Santa took from his meager sack three small, beautifully-wrapped packages, and proceeded to randomly distribute the gifts to the audience. I happened to receive one of the packages and was asked to open it. I carefully unwrapped the parcel, only to find the box empty. The wise Santa asked me what I had received as my gift. I replied, "My gift is empty; there is nothing here." He responded, "That's right, because the greatest gift is the one you give away, not the one you receive. What would be the gift you would most want to give away?" I thought for several seconds and finally said, "Love. I would like to give *love* to everyone I meet." With that response the Santa moved to the recipient of the next gift without saying another word to me.

The second participant was asked to open his package, which yielded the same empty result. The wise Santa asked him the same question and his answer was, "Hope. I would like to give the people I meet *hope*." Without speaking, Santa moved to the third participant and inquired of him the present he would like to give. His reply was, "Faith. I would like to give *faith*."

All three gift holders had spoken from their hearts, and the responses made us ponder the impact of what we had just witnessed. The Swedish Santa quietly began to speak. "In our country, when we visit the children, we do not ask them what they would **like** for Christmas. Instead, we ask them what they would **give** their family and loved ones. We teach them the real joy of Christmas comes from giving, instead of receiving, and the greatest gifts are those given from your own heart, like "Love, Hope and Faith."

What a simple, yet profound lesson for all of us American Santas. In a land of "I want, I want, I want," perhaps we have lost what Christmas *really* is all about. This lesson has influenced my role as Santa Claus ever since witnessing it.

My wife told me a similar story about her mother a few years after we were married. The incident didn't happen at Christmas, but the occurrence had a message about giving.

Janie is one of six sisters and while she was growing up, her parents had to work really hard to provide for their family. They lived in the city but had gardens all around their neighborhood (and at relatives), wherever a patch of ground could be found to grow a few vegetables. They even raised their own chickens to provide eggs and an occasional chicken dinner. My wife just assumed that was the way all families got by.

It was Janie's mother's custom to wait until she could buy all of her girls something they needed before buying them anything individually. If dresses were on sale, each girl got a new dress if funds were available. (Otherwise, "hand-me-downs had to work.)

One particular Sunday at church, when the offering was being taken, Janie saw her mother reach for her purse. She watched her take all the money in her wallet and put it into the plate. Knowing that she needed new shoes before school started, Janie looked at her mother in wonderment.

After the family Sunday dinner that afternoon, Janie mustered up the courage to say to her mother, "I thought you were going to buy me new school shoes; why did you put all of your money in the church offering?" Her mother's wise reply was, "All of you girls need new shoes and I didn't have enough money to buy them, so I asked God to provide a way, and He will." That was the end of the discussion.

That story has had a great impact on my life, both as an example of faith and to the importance of tithing. It reminds me of the story of the widow's mite in the Bible.

I wish I could say I have lived my life by examples such as these. Sadly, at Christmas time, I'm often so caught up in the excitement of my role as Santa Claus, that I sometimes forget that I can't grant everyone's wish, or even anyone's. At those times, my memory and my heart help me realize I *can* give the gift of unconditional love to everyone. I *can* rely on my own faith in God and humankind and try to impart faith to others. I *can* share the gift of hope, both for myself as well as our troubled world, that, somehow, these priceless gifts *are* the greatest of all.

It was Christ himself who said, "Faith, hope and love, these three remain. But the greatest of these is Love."

Santa Was a Boy Scout

Do you ever wonder how Santa Claus manages to survive all the cold winter trips he has to make in his sleigh every Christmas Eve? He was a Boy Scout!

It's amazing the things I know how to do by learning them as a Boy Scout. I remember well the camping trips and hikes; learning, the hard way, to dress for all types of weather conditions. I learned how to keep a fire burning, even in the rain, and how to cook a meal with the strangest ingredients, and enjoy it like it was a feast (maybe because I was so hungry). I learned how to tie a knot for any need…which has really come in handy when replacing lost bells on my boots.

Throughout my entire scouting career, my goal was to become an Eagle Scout. Somehow I felt any young man who achieved that rank proved himself worthy of stepping into manhood. I had all of the required merit badges, except "physical fitness." I just could not, no matter how hard I tried, do six pull-ups, and I still can't!

Along my journey toward the elusive rank of Eagle Scout, I did, however, accomplish other important goals. One of the requirements for the God and Country award is to learn the books of the Bible from memory. I can still recite most of them in order, and find that quite helpful in looking up Biblical references today.

Becoming a member of the Order of the Arrow (an honor bestowed upon Boy Scouts by their fellow members), taught me many more life lessons. Enduring hardship and practicing self-denial was necessary to attain "Ordeal" status.

The values of service to my fellow scouts and the rest of mankind were learned while becoming a "Brotherhood" member. Finally, being able to endure mandatory imposed isolation with self-sufficiency, I was honored to become a full "Vigil" member. It was then I was given my own Indian name, taken from the language of the Lenape Indians. My name is "Amangi," which means "Big." What an appropriate name for Santa Claus!

My love for wildlife was developed while being a Boy Scout. I had encounters with deer, bears, eagles, hawks, snakes, turtles, raccoons, ducks, squirrels and even skunks. Each has uniqueness according to God's creative design, and they deserve to live in their environment just as much as we do. To this day, I cannot even think of harming any creature. I am fascinated by each animal's beauty, and that is why only recycled furs (found in antique shops) adorn my Santa Claus suits.

My true appreciation for the Boy Scout organization was brought full circle after becoming a Scout leader myself. When our son, Rob, became old enough to become a Boy Scout, we tried all sorts of things to get him interested in the program. I took him to meetings, but he just wasn't impressed. I shared my patch collection with him (because he was the ultimate collector), but he still wasn't interested.

Finally, in 1982, we had the opportunity to travel to Los Angeles to introduce a National Environmental Stamp for Keep America Beautiful. The conservation stamp featured a portrait of Iron Eyes Cody, the "crying Indian," who appeared on television commercials for the organization in the 1970s and 1980s. Iron Eyes appeared with us at in the Los Angeles Convention Center, where he signed autographs for hundreds of people making donations to Keep America Beautiful so they could get the collectible stamp.

During our visit to Los Angeles, Mr. Cody invited my family to his home in Griffith Park, a suburb of Hollywood, where he was employed as an actor. Walking into his modest home was like walking into a museum of Native American arts and crafts. We were all mesmerized by the artifacts he had collected, or had been given, from many tribes and nations.

A Native American custom is to give a gift of friendship to visitors in your home. He gave each of us a special memento of our visit. Iron Eyes' gift to me was an eagle feather he had worn in his hair. (He had told us he was part Cherokee and part Cree Indian.) The Cree would wear a single eagle feather as adornment which actually became our friend's trademark. He even gave me a card documenting the feather's provenance, since only Native Americans are allowed to possess feathers from endangered birds of prey.

The most life-changing gift Iron Eyes presented, however, was a miniature tom-tom he gave to our son. The gesture itself impressed Rob so much that he listened as Mr. Cody talked about his own involvement with the Boy Scouts and what a great organization he thought it was. When we arrived back in North Carolina, one evening Rob asked me, "Dad, do you think we could go to a Boy Scout meeting?"

As the saying goes, "The rest is history!" Rob became a Boy Scout and I volunteered as his Scoutmaster. We formed Troop 77 at our church. (Ironically, I had belonged to Troop 7 as a scout, so Troop 77 seemed like a significant continuation of my scouting career – a "perfect" number in a way). I finally, by proxy, achieved my Eagle Scout "goal" by pinning the award on my son's chest five years later. Seeing his success, and being a part of it, was the greatest reward I could have ever received. Together, we graduated six more Eagle Scouts before a fractured hip ended my camping days.

Some of my greatest lessons from Boy Scouts involved the mentoring of young men by older adults. I still admire and respect the scout leaders who took the time to work with and guide me when I needed it. They became father figures, standing in for my dad who died in 1962. As Scoutmaster to my son, and the fifty or so other young men who joined our troop, I tried to pass on to them the nurturing and guidance I had received. I don't know how much influence I had on them, but I do know *they* played an important part in making me who I am today; hopefully, a man worthy of the responsible role of Santa Claus.

Santa Visits a Karaoke Bar

Every year I spend a few days with several talented photographers who arrange appointments with clients that want their photo taken with Santa. I always enjoy these sessions. Many of the children have come for several years and it has been fun to see them grow up. I always look forward to the time as much as they do, and we get some wonderful photographs.

A few years ago, after a long day of shooting at one such event, I met with some friends at a restaurant near my motel. The restaurant was called Fat Boys (an appropriate place to find Santa) and they specialized in barbecued ribs. After a great evening of food and fellowship, one of my friends suggested we go to the back of the restaurant where they had a karaoke bar.

I remember thinking to myself, "Santa can't go into a bar! I don't drink any kind of alcoholic beverages; what would people think about seeing me in a bar?" Then I thought again, "Why not have fun with my friends? I can be the same person in a bar that I am anywhere else. I don't have to have alcohol to drink; I can just sit and enjoy the singing." You should have heard all of the cheers and greetings when we entered. Everyone was glad to see Santa. They patted me on the back, gave me "high-fives" and welcomed me like I was someone special.

While greeting everyone, and a little embarrassed at all the attention, a little boy of about six or seven years of age, wearing a red toboggan suddenly came running up to me yelling, "Santa, Santa, you came to see me!" With that greeting, he jumped up into my arms and gave me a great big hug. After enjoying his hug, and trying to put him down, he wanted to stay in my arms; so with him holding on, I made my way to the side of the stage to find a seat. Once seated, I asked the little boy what his name was and what he wanted for Christmas.

Jeffrey was a slightly-built youngster and looked rather pale, as though he had been sick; but nothing hampered his enthusiasm. As far as he was concerned, he was having a visit with his own personal Santa Claus. After we had talked for several minutes, he jumped out of my lap and disappeared into the crowd. I composed myself and started enjoying the show. After a little while, Jeffrey returned with a glass of iced tea and some peanuts that he had fixed, just for Santa. I later found out his mother was a waitress at the bar, and the only way she could come to work was to bring Jeffrey with her.

Seemingly happy to just sit in my lap, Jeffrey and I enjoyed the music together. I was content to have him with me because he made me feel less self-conscious about being "in a bar." After awhile, Jeffrey began to intermittently jump down, leave, be gone for awhile, and then come back. Each time, upon returning, he would hug me again. His hugs were unlike any I had ever had...like he had found his very best friend, who loved him unconditionally and whom he loved, even if it was just for a few hours on a Friday night in the middle of a karaoke bar.

Jeffrey's mother came over and said she would ask him to leave me alone if I wanted her to, but I was enjoying him as much as he was enjoying me. A little later another waitress came over and told me that Jeffrey had a brain tumor and was being treated with radiation. What I had sensed was true; here was a child with a special need. There were three other children there that night, but they were too busy singing karaoke to care much about Santa Claus;

although they did sing "Here Comes Santa Claus" for my enjoyment and the other revelers.

But for Jeffrey, on that special night, God had sent him his own personal Santa Claus to spend time with. And to think, I almost didn't go into that bar thinking it wasn't a "place for Santa." The lesson for me was you can be the person you are wherever you find yourself.

The Story Continues, 2006...

Once again this year, I enjoyed visiting with my photographer friend and his wonderful clients. After a long day of shooting, I decided to visit Fat Boys alone for dinner. It had been several years since that special visit with Jeffrey. Everyone seemed glad to see Santa, and several children stopped by my table to visit with me.

After finishing my meal, I asked my waitress if she could tell me how Jeffrey was doing, (relating the story from my previous visit). She confessed she had not been there long and went to get another waitress, who had worked there for more than fifteen years. After recounting my story to her, she said she was not aware of a waitress who would have worked there with a son named Jeffrey, and her manager confirmed that fact.

Perhaps I had been "entertaining an angel unaware". If so, I am very satisfied to leave it at that.

Santa's Coat of Many Colors

A few years ago while cleaning out the attic; I found a plastic bag with a carefully-folded handmade quilt inside. As I unwrapped and unfolded the treasure, I realized it was a "crazy quilt," a colorful collection of different fabric scraps; silks from old neckties and handkerchiefs, cotton from dresses, and wool from suits, pieced together randomly to form a heavy blanket. I took it to my mother's house (yes! Santa has a mother too) and asked if she recognized it. She said, "Yes, your grandmother made it with the help of your great-grandmother."

I took the quilt home and thought for several days about what to do with it. It was quite worn in some areas, where the fabrics weren't as sturdy as others. Careful examination revealed a few patches with beautiful embroidered flowers and geometric designs. I could just imagine my grandmother saving the scraps of her family's past garments and then carefully and artistically crafting them into a useful covering.

The quilt brought back fond memories of my grandmother. She started her married life as a school teacher in a one-room schoolhouse in upstate New York. My grandfather managed the family farm that had been established in 1812. "Mammy," as we grandchildren called her, was a diminutive woman, barely standing five feet tall − but to her children and my grandfather − she was in charge. Every summer, when her children were out of school, she insisted they begin *and* finish a summer project. My mother remembers quilting and other sewing as her main summer pastime. To this day, my mother, who is 89 years old, knits sweaters, shawls, baby hats and booties, and then donates them to hospitals and nursing homes. She even helps teach other ladies in our church how to knit, meeting with them two Saturdays each month. Her mother taught her well.

I took the crazy quilt to my seamstress, Eva Rae Clark (who is a retired school teacher herself,) and asked her if she could make a Santa's cloak out of it. In astonishment she exclaimed, "You're not going to cut *that* up, are you?!" After I explained to her that I would think more often of my grandmother while wearing her handiwork as a garment than I would putting it away, or even using it on a bed, she understood my desires. She then, in her school-teacher manner replied, "We will have to be like a good carpenter, and measure twice before we cut!"

For several weeks during that summer, I got together with my seamstress and tried on a muslin pattern of the cloak before she actually cut the quilt. We also examined several fur coats (found in antique shops), looking for an appropriate trim for the garment. Finally we decided on a dark, mink fur, and the transformation began to take place. Once the quilt was cut, there was enough of it left for a complementing shawl collar, a hat, and shoulder bag in which to carry Santa's treats.

By that time, *our little project* had caught the attention of neighbors and even our local TV station, which eventually aired a story about "Santa's Coat of Many Colors." When the day finally arrived for my official fitting of the new attire, I was completely overwhelmed with emotion as I put on the cloak. It was perfect in every way. Even the original regal, satin quilt backing my grandmother had used worked perfectly as the robe's lining. It all came together and complimented the Santa suit Ms. Clark had made for me the previous year.

To me, the cloak stands for exactly what a handmade quilt should represent – the warmth and love of family, and the stewardship of using what we have to make something useful. I had a sense that my grandmother would be proud of me, as the "summer project" I had chosen for myself was a complete success.

Santa's Christmas Castle

Did you know that Santa has his own castle? In 2006 I decided I needed a more "southern" satellite base of operations, where the elves could manufacture toys, and where Mrs. Claus and I could receive visitors.

In 1832 a young man named Charles McCulloch discovered gold in the piedmont region of North Carolina near the village of Jamestown. Upon his discovery, a North Carolina "gold rush" began and the Scotsman decided to build a fortress to both protect his discovery, and as a place to refine the gold he mined. Castle McCulloch, as the structure is known today, was fashioned after the European castles with solid granite walls quarried right on the site. The huge chimney, for the smelting furnace, became the focal point of the structure; the water from the property was directed through the castle to separate the gold nuggets from the river silt and rocks of the countryside.

After the discovery of gold in California in 1849, most of the remaining miners left North Carolina to seek their fortune in the Gold Rush out west. The McCulloch family followed, leaving the building abandoned. During America's Civil War, the castle was used as a hospital for southern soldiers before they were transported to hospitals in Richmond, Virginia.

As the century turned into the 1900s, the castle fell victim to vandals; eventually nothing was left standing of the magnificent structure except the massive chimney. Many local residents didn't even know there had been a castle in that hardwood forest.

In the 1970s another enterprising entrepreneur named Richard Harris heard about a site where a castle had once stood and began to inquire about its location. Eventually he was able to purchase the property (and about sixty additional acres) and set about to single-handedly rebuild the structure. Since I live in the area, I became aware of Mr. Harris' project and of the rumors that he was a "dreamer" with ideas larger than his resources. Being a successful mechanical engineer by training, the preservationist began to reconstruct the castle to the exact specifications of the original building. Many of the granite stones were still lying around on the site, having been toppled over by vandals, but too heavy to haul away. However, hundreds more had to be hand chiseled before the job was completed.

The trees on the property were not large enough to yield the timbers for the massive beams and walls needed to support the stonework. Mr. Harris traveled to neighboring Randolph County, where he used primitive saw mill techniques to cut down ancient trees and fashion them into support beams for the structure. Then he left the timbers in the lumber yard curing for two years before beginning his construction of the building.

Meanwhile, the visionary continued to recover the building stones and collected local slate for the castle floors. The cedar shakes for the roof were all hand-cut on the property. Feeling that every castle needs a moat, Mr. Harris redirected a local stream to surround the structure. He created ponds adjacent to one side of the building and what he would call "Crystal Lake" in front of the castle.

The castle itself consists of almost 7,000 square feet, including a Grand Entry Ball Room accessible from the drawbridge in front of the castle, through two massive twenty-foot-tall doors. This area houses a banquet hall with adjoining serving rooms and a kitchen. Below the banquet room are two large rooms that can be used for additional dining areas. (Mr. Harris' original goal was to fashion Castle McCulloch into a fine European five-star restaurant and reception hall.)

I don't remember exactly when I first met Richard Harris, but I do remember being immediately captivated by his vision and drive to "live out his dream." He enthusiastically explained everything that had taken place up to the point of having Castle McCulloch designated as a National Historic Treasure Landmark.

After becoming a naturally-bearded Santa Claus in 1995, I was invited to a Christmas wedding at Castle McCulloch. The bride wanted Santa there to greet her guests during the reception. The Queen's Chamber, where the wedding guests would be received, was beautifully decorated with its own Christmas tree and there were special treats for all of the guests. The thought occurred to me, "What a wonderful place Castle McCulloch would be for Santa and 'Mrs. Claus' to live."

In June, 2006, a call came from the public-relations director of Castle McCulloch. She had been referred to me by a former neighbor who knew of my portrayal as Santa Claus. The young lady asked if I would be interested in talking to them about a new Christmas event they were planning. It had been over ten years since my last visit to the Castle, so I was eager to hear about their new plans.

The idea of "Christmas Castle" captured me the first day while being reacquainted with the owner. I felt as though I was in the presence of a modern-day P. T. Barnum, as Mr. Harris became animated, enthusiastically describing all his plans and dreams. He envisioned the new endeavor as, one day, becoming the premier holiday attraction in the state and perhaps, eventually, the entire Southeast.

Christmas Castle was planned as a night-time attraction featuring a walk through "Santa's Enchanted Forest." There, guests would encounter almost fifty costumed characters including "Mother Goose," magicians, jugglers, singers, dancers, storytellers, the Grinch and even Santa's elves. Original songs were written to the score of familiar Christmas tunes, and the entire event was choreographed by a professional community theater director.

Continuing on, guests could enter "Santa's Christmas Castle," where a giant 22-foot musical Christmas tree would greet them. After walking through the Great Hall of the castle, guests were to be greeted by "Mrs. Claus" and her display of old-world figurines depicting Santa. In an adjoining room, a spirited Mariachi band would be playing. Next, the visitors would exit the castle through the back entrance and proceed into the underground toy shop where the elves were busy making toys.

After enjoying cookies and hot chocolate, made by the elves, visitors could visit with Santa in his throne room. Yes, it was the very same room I had visited during the wedding reception twelve years previously. Santa's throne itself was on a raised granite pedestal in an octagonal bay window overlooking the castle moat. The leaded panes of the window encase colorful stained glass. Seated on the leather and mahogany hand-carved throne, I had a chance to visit with each guest while photographer elves snapped our picture.

Christmas Castle was an immediate success; over thirteen thousand people visited during our first season. For me, it was a wonderful opportunity to see my Santa career come to such a grand juncture. The very place I once visited and dreamed about being "Santa's Castle" had actually become just what I had envisioned.

One evening after Christmas, Mr. Harris and I were standing outside the castle as the sun was going down and the lights were beginning to sparkle through the woods. He said, "You know, Santa, I could have sold this property several years ago for more than I would have thought possible, but then I wouldn't have had a dream to keep me going. Christmas Castle has been my dream, just like being Santa Claus has been your dream. Without a dream, life can be pretty boring. What do you say that you and I live out our dreams here at Christmas Castle?"

Sleigh Bells

There is something about the sound of *real* sleigh bells that has always transported me right into the Christmas spirit. The makers of real sleigh bells, like those on Santa's team of reindeer, forge graduated sizes of bells, each with its own unique sound. When mounted onto a harness for horses or reindeer to wear, the various sized bells create an orchestra of beautifully pitched notes.

Once I became Santa, I wanted my own set of sleigh bells so I could experience the sound *he* hears firsthand. During one of my visits to an old country store in rural North Carolina, I actually found an antique harness of bells mounted on a leather strap with a buckle on one end. Since the strap was made to fit a horse, it was large enough to fit around my waist. The bells were black with tarnish and the leather was stiff and cracked. The owner of the store was surprised at my interest in the old bells, especially when I offered to buy them.

On and off, for several weeks after returning home with my purchase, I polished each bell and worked saddle soap into the leather harness. To be honest, the belt had to be shortened a little − thankfully my girth wasn't quite equal to that of a horse! After finishing my project, I had a beautiful belt which could be worn with my Santa suit. However, after wearing it a few times, I realized there was no way to sneak up on anyone wearing those bells! Everyone could hear Santa coming because with every step the bells would ring. So when quiet is needed, the bells stay home.

One year, when my granddaughter, Carrie, was about five years old, she and her family were at our home on Christmas Eve. Carrie was so excited we couldn't get her to go to bed, so we told her Santa couldn't come until she was asleep. While everyone was encouraging her to head for bed, I took my sleigh-bell belt and went outside, unnoticed. I rushed around to the front of our house shaking the sleigh bells. My family later told me Carrie shot right off for the bedroom frantically yelling, "He's here! Santa's here! I have to go to bed!" She didn't come out until the next morning.

Years ago, a few men from my church began meeting once a week for prayer and fellowship. Every week at 6:00 on Thursday mornings, we would meet at various places, share our individual concerns, and then pray for each other and our families. Eventually other responsibilities and priorities led all but two of us in different directions. Over time, we have forged a friendship that has carried us through our children growing into adulthood and the birth of all my grandchildren. We have shared tremendous joy and unspeakable sorrow during the almost twenty years of our continued, Thursday morning fellowship. That bond of friendship is one of the things I treasure most.

A few years ago, my good friend was hosting a Christmas party at his home and asked if Santa could make a surprise visit during the evening. After several visits at other locations during that night, I made the final stop at my friend's house. He answered the front door and announced my "surprise" arrival. Upon entering his home, I heard the sound of sleigh bells. There on the doorknob was one of the most beautiful hand-forged set of sleigh bells I had ever seen. I carried on about how wonderful the bells sounded and then proceeded to wish everyone a "Merry Christmas!" After a short period of fellowship and wonderful food, Santa bid everyone a "Good night!"

Since the two of us exchange Christmas gifts each year on the Thursday before Christmas, I've grown to anticipate that day just like "a kid at Christmas." Witnessing my transformation into Santa Claus, my friend's gifts have, in many ways, acknowledged that part of my personality. The year I "crashed" his party, my gift from him was the very set of sleigh bells I had admired on his front door. It was not a set *like* the one he had, but *those* very bells which had been a part of his family's Christmas celebration for years.

Those beautiful bells now hang all year on the door of my home. Each time I see and hear them, I think of our priceless friendship. I don't leave my house as Santa Claus without "Nelson's sleigh bells." They announce my presence as I enter a room, (and even vicinity) and they set the tone for a special Christmas celebration.

My Sleigh Ride

One highlight of the Charles W. Howard Santa Claus School in Midland, Michigan is the trip to see "Santa's sleigh." The dean of the school has built the ultimate Santa Claus float. He has constructed a massive sleigh on a forty-foot-long, flat-bed trailer. Built of beautiful honey-colored oak and pine, there is a seat for Santa and a back seat full of toys with his bag on top. A green railroad lantern is on the right of the sleigh and a red one is on the left.

Each student gets the opportunity to mount the sleigh, and while cameras flash, take his "fantasy ride." It takes a fifteen-foot step ladder to help Santa mount his vehicle. Once settled in the seat, he can pick up the reins which are attached to a full team of reindeer – all eight of them plus Rudolph. These are not the usual plastic or fiberglass reindeer you see in most Christmas parades. No, they are full-sized reindeer made with wire-mesh bodies and covered with faux fur. The steeds are mounted on individual suspension springs which bounce when Santa shakes the reins, thus giving the appearance that the team is running. The reins have built-in lights as well as a personalized harness on each reindeer. With Rudolph's nose lit to lead the way, the whole scene is right out of "The Night before Christmas." There is no feeling like the rush that surges through you when you shake the reins and watch the reindeer take off right before your eyes.

There are a few fortunate Santas who have their own sleighs and some even have their own reindeer. One of the photographers I work with has one, and the children love to sit in it with me. I also know a man in Tennessee who raises real reindeer. (I even have a set of naturally-shed antlers from one of them in my Santa Claus house). I invited him to bring his team of reindeer to Christmas Castle, but North Carolina quarantine laws won't allow reindeer into our state.

Tom and Holly Valent, the operators of the C. W. Howard Santa Claus School, have a pair of reindeer at their home in Michigan. They live in a Norwegian-styled barn behind their owner's house. It's quite an experience petting and talking to a live reindeer. They are magnificent animals and you can't help but fall in love with them when you look into their beautiful brown eyes. Both the male and female reindeer have impressive antlers which grow new each year. Sometimes the growth doesn't necessarily coincide with the Christmas season, but that is a minor detail. I say, "If they can fly on Christmas Eve, they can always have their antlers at Christmas too!"

I don't know if I will ever have the opportunity to experience a sleigh ride pulled by a team of reindeer, but, I have the assurance in my heart I will one day take my "sleigh ride" to heaven. I know that because God has forgiven me of my sins through my personal confession and acceptance of His Son, Jesus Christ, as my Savior; thus guaranteeing that assurance.

Talk about a "Merry Christmas!" Can you imagine the holiday celebration that will take place there?

Why I Believe in Santa Claus

"For God so loved the world, that He gave His only begotten Son, that whosoever believeth in Him should not perish, but shall have everlasting life."

John 3:16

That verse in the Bible, the simple message of salvation, is the reason we celebrate Christmas. God was the giver of the most incredible gift, not to be matched throughout the rest of history. Each year people all over the world celebrate that gift at Christmas time. Some celebrate the gift in their own hearts through acceptance of the Christ of Christmas, while others just enjoy the season of giving.

Another man, Nicholas of Myra, in the fourth century, acknowledged his sins also and became a believer in Christ. He eventually became canonized as a saint – Saint Nicholas; the inspiration of all who have followed in his footsteps as Santa Claus. It is the spirit of Saint Nicholas that lives in the hearts of all *true* Santas, just like the spirit of Christ lives in the hearts of all true Christians

It is not my responsibility to prove either of the facts I have just described to anyone. I can only attempt to live my life in such a way that it may serve as an example, a lamp-post perhaps, of the Spirit living within me. If I allow God's Spirit to live and work through me, then I can experience the gift of Christmas every day of the year. More importantly, if I can somehow share the love God has showered on me with those who I come in contact with, then my life will truly be blessed and perhaps their lives will be too.

"Merry Christmas to All,
and to All a Good Night!"

Santa Cliff

About the Author

Cliff Snider is a husband, father, and grandfather who for the last forty-five years has spent most Christmases dressed as Santa Claus. In his *real* life he assists artists in the production and marketing of their creative efforts. In *Santa's Journey*, the shadow-artist applies his own voice and hand to his creative side. The author resides with his wife, Janie, in North Carolina where he is the signature Santa for Christmas Castle in Jamestown, in an authentic 1832 medieval castle. In 2007, Cliff's story, "It Must Be Santa" was featured in *Our State* magazine and his story of "The Praying Santa" aired on *The 700 Club* on Christmas Day.

About the Artist

Many people spend their lives doing things they don't enjoy and never find their special place in life. Wendy Leedy has touched people's hearts through her artwork and freely gives the glory to God.

A graduate of the University of Tennessee with a degree in Fine Art, her interest in horses and art has opened doors for her. She served as art director for *The Voice of the Tennessee Walking Horse* magazine, and her first published artwork appeared on the cover. She has more than 80 published calendars to her credit, and has won numerous awards with her drawings.

She owns and operates The Frame House in Bean Station, Tennessee and lives with her husband, Buford Watson, in nearby Blaine, where they raise Paint horses and beef cattle. Wendy has found her special place in life.